The Flourishing Principal

Also in the It's Easy to W.R.I.T.E. Expressive Writing Series

Expressive Writing: Foundations of Practice
Kathleen Adams, Editor

The Teachers Journal: A Workbook for Self-Discovery
Kathleen Adams and Marisé Barreiro

The Flourishing Principal

Strategies for Self-Renewal

KATHLEEN ADAMS AND
ROSEMARY LOHNDORF

ROWMAN & LITTLEFIELD EDUCATION
A Division of
ROWMAN & LITTLEFIELD PUBLISHERS, INC.
Lanham • New York • Toronto • Plymouth, UK

Published by Rowman & Littlefield Education
A division of Rowman & Littlefield Publishers, Inc.
A wholly owned subsidiary of The Rowman & Littlefield Publishing Group, Inc.
4501 Forbes Boulevard, Suite 200, Lanham, Maryland 20706
www.rowman.com

10 Thornbury Road, Plymouth PL6 7PP, United Kingdom

British Library Cataloguing in Publication Information Available

Library of Congress Cataloging-in-Publication Data

Adams, Kathleen, 1951-

The flourishing principal : strategies for self-renewal / Kathleen Adams and Rosemary Lohndorf.

pages cm

Includes bibliographical references.

ISBN 978-1-4758-0296-2 (pbk. : alk. paper) — ISBN 978-1-4758-0297-9 (electronic)

1. School principals—Psychology. 2. School principals—Attitudes. 3. Education—Authorship. 4. Diaries—Authorship. 5. Self-actualization (Psychology)—Problems, exercises, etc. I. Title.

LB2831.9.A43 2013

371.2'012—dc23

201300989

∞™ The paper used in this publication meets the minimum requirements of American National Standard for Information Sciences—Permanence of Paper for Printed Library Materials, ANSI/NISO Z39.48-1992.

Printed in the United States of America

Dedicated to

Robb Jackson, Ph.D., CJF, CAPF
1952–2013

You will go out in joy
and be led forth in peace;
the mountains and hills
will burst into song before you,
and all the trees of the field
will clap their hands.
Isaiah 55:12, NIV

Contents

Series Overview About the *It's Easy to W.R.I.T.E.* Expressive Writing Series

Expressive writing originates from the writer's lived experience—past, present, or imagined future. Written in the author's own voice, expressive writing creates bridges between thought and feeling, reason and intuition, idea and action. It is equally rooted in language arts and social science, and it takes multiple forms: journals, poetry, life story, personal essay, creative nonfiction, song lyrics, notes, and snippets of thought. Expressive writing is democratic and accessible. No special knowledge is needed, supplies are available and affordable, and research confirms that outcomes can be profound and even life changing.

The *It's Easy to W.R.I.T.E.* Expressive Writing Series captures the voices of worldwide experts on the power of writing for personal development, academic improvement, and lasting behavioral change. Authors are both theorists and practitioners of the work they document, bringing real-life examples of practical techniques and stories of actual outcomes.

Individually or as a compendium, the volumes in the *It's Easy to W.R.I.T.E.* Expressive Writing Series represent thoughtful, innovative, demonstrated approaches to the myriad ways life-based writing can shape both critical thinking and emotional intelligence. Books in the series are designed to have versatile appeal for classroom teachers and administrators, health and behavioral health professionals, graduate programs that prepare educators and counselors, facilitators of expressive writing, and individuals who themselves write expressively. Workbooks offer well-crafted, self-paced writing programs for individual users, with facilitation guides and curricula for anyone who wishes to organize peer-writing circles to explore the material in community.

Each book or chapter author is held to exacting standards set by the series editor, Kathleen Adams, who, prior to her 1985 launch as a pioneer and global expert in the expressive writing field, was trained as a journalist and served as chief editor for a nonfiction publishing company.

It's Easy to W.R.I.T.E.

What do you want to write about? Name it. Write it down. (If you don't know, try one of these: *What's going on? How do I feel? What's on my mind? What do I want? What's the most important thing to do? What's the best/worst thing right now?*)

Reconnect with your center. Close your eyes. Take three deep breaths. Focus. Relax your body and mind. Gather your thoughts, feelings, questions, ideas.

Investigate your thoughts and feelings. Start writing and keep writing. Follow the pen/keyboard. If you get stuck, close your eyes and recenter yourself. Reread what you've already written and continue. Try not to edit as you go; that can come later, if at all.

Time yourself. Write for five to twenty minutes or whatever time you choose. Set the timer on your phone, stove, or computer. Plan another three to five minutes at the end for reflection.

Exit smart. Reread what you've written and reflect on it in a sentence or two: *As I read this, I notice . . .* or *I'm aware of . . .* or *I feel . . .* Note any action steps you might take or any prompts you might use for additional writes.

Preface

This workbook was germinated in a week-long facilitator training that I taught in the spring of 2012. My coauthor, Rosemary Lohndorf, was participating in an intensive course to become certified as an instructor of a journal writing course I developed. I knew from her application that she was recently retired as a primary school principal in Colorado's Boulder Valley School District. As we progressed through the week, I also learned that she was a woman of thoughtful, discerning voice and mind. She was both authentically vulnerable and authentically self-reliant. She understood the power of writing and had been using it for years to come to her own clarity and alignment. As one who makes art, dances, and writes to communicate with herself and others, Rosemary also embodied the spirit and soul of a creative.

Some months earlier my editor had suggested an expressive writing workbook for school principals who juggle nonstop demands, often at the expense of their own physical, emotional, and relational well-being. I was holding the idea expectantly, receptive to meeting a principal who embodied the profound revelatory and healing powers of expressive writing. As I observed Rosemary in action and conversed with her over meals, I knew I had found my coauthor.

At that point, the only other thing I knew was that I wanted to offer a guided writing program that relied on a strengths-based approach to self-renewal. With that frame in place, Rosemary and I instantly aligned on several concepts, among them the importance of core values, creativity, balance, and self-care. I filled in other flourishing concepts from my twenty-five years of experience as a strengths-based, solution-focused psychotherapist. Rosemary wrote dozens of stories from her training and career as a principal, and she combed her journals for examples that illustrated the ways she flourished, or failed to.

If you are new to expressive writing, we hope you'll find this workbook to be a deep dive into the many ways writing can help you clarify your thinking, open your minds and hearts to authentic voice, and experience the relief of release.

If you are a new principal, we hope that you will find in Rosemary a role model and exemplar whose experiences can guide you into your own exploration.

If you are starting to fray under the unrelenting demands of heading a school, we hope that you will find refreshing insight and practical guidance for befriending your flourishing self.

If you find yourself dangerously close to burnout because of values-conflicting "marching orders" from the people and institutions to which you are accountable—the school board, administrators, superintendents, districts, unions—we hope this workbook will give language to your conflicts and deepen your own recognition of True North.

If your principalship is a source of fulfillment and your school is thriving, we hope that you will find it gratifying and inspirational to document your own best practice.

This work is powerful when done alone, and it's even more powerful in community. You'll find a facilitator's guide at the back of the book, complete with a suggested outline for developing a group process out of chapters 2 through 12. Invite some colleagues to join you in a *Flourishing Principal* writing group. Surprise and delight and inspire each other.

May your writing and your work be blessed!

Kathleen Adams
May 2013

1

Why Write?

How This Workbook Can Help You

When I was ten years old, I discovered the magic of writing down my life. I started with the little locking five-year diary—a feminine "write of passage" in the 1960s. In middle school I graduated to a Big Chief tablet and a purple ballpoint pen. Over the years, I have filled hundreds, maybe thousands, of notebooks and journals.

Writing down my thoughts, feelings, questions, concerns, dreams, confessions, and inspirations has been a major contributor to the development of my emotional intelligence, problem-solving abilities, and healthy self-concept. My journals and notebooks are curious, receptive friends with the tireless capacity to mirror truth and understanding.

The social science research initiated by preeminent research psychologist James W. Pennebaker and others demonstrate that expressive writing helps improve both physiological and psychological well-being. There are various theories as to how and why this happens, but in general there is agreement that writing authentically about one's own lived experience helps construct a coherent, consistent narrative and assists in finding meaning in life's challenges and difficulties (Pennebaker and Beall 1986; Pennebaker 1989, 2004; Smyth 1998; Frattaroli 2006). My own research indicates that expressive writing offers clarity and insight, promotes emotional management through safe, effective catharsis of feelings, accelerates the resolution of difficulties, and helps manage stress (Adams 2013).

Although much of the formal research focuses on writing about traumatic or highly stressful matters, it is not necessary to write about deeply troubling material in order to derive the benefit. In a 2012 study, volunteers were asked to write in a structured way four times over the course of a week about "everyday normal" problems. Nearly all made significant shifts in their attitudes about and behaviors regarding the problem (Adams 2013).

Maybe, in the course of this workbook, you'll activate strengths that have been buried under layers of exhaustion, tension, or stress. Maybe you'll recognize the intricacies of synchronicity, serendipity, or just plain luck in your self-renewal process. Perhaps the sun will break through the fog of unknowing and illuminate the creative, energetic teacher on the other side. Perhaps you'll articulate your own best practice in a way that shines lights of insight and wisdom.

Possibly you'll come together in community and write with your peers, sharing stories with the sort of authentic self-discovery that is uncommon in the crowded halls and groaning calendars of the workday.

Whatever your individual outcomes and results, Rosemary and I sincerely hope that you will emerge from the other side of this workbook refreshed and even inspired by a deepened sense of your innate resources, uniquely your own, that lead you to a triumph of self-renewal.

Kay

It's Easy to W.R.I.T.E.

Try these five easy steps. You'll be writing!

W What do you want to write about? Name it. (Some options, if you're not writing from a prompt: What's going on? How do you feel? What are you thinking about? What do you want? What's the best thing and the worst thing going on right now?)

R Reconnect with your center. Close your eyes. Take three deep breaths. Focus. Relax your body and mind. Gather your thoughts, feelings, and questions about the writing prompt you're starting with, or the story with which you'll begin.

I Investigate your thoughts and feelings. Start writing and keep writing. Follow the pen/keyboard. If you get stuck or run out of juice, close your eyes and recenter yourself. Reread what you've already written and continue.

T Time yourself. Write for five to twenty minutes, depending on the complexity of the topic. Warm-ups and reflections can typically be completed in three to five minutes; the main writes in each chapter will benefit from ten to fifteen minutes.

E Exit smart by rereading what you've written and reflecting on it in a sentence or two: *As I read this, I notice* . . . or *I'm aware of* . . . or *I feel* . . . Note any action steps you might take. Space is designated at the end of each chapter for an overall reflection. You may also want to reflect after each main write, as it is a surprisingly effective pathway to clarity and insight.

Suggestions for Satisfying Writing

Since there are no "rules" (correct spelling and grammar, handwriting vs. computer, etc.) for expressive writing, it's hard to make a mistake! However, many people benefit from keeping these suggestions in mind.

1. **Be mindful of privacy.** Discreetly stash your notebook (or this book, if you're using the writing space provided) in its own special place (book bag, nightstand, desk drawer) for peace of mind and protection from curious eyes. If you're writing on a computer, give your files nondescriptive names that you can decode.

2. **Start by centering.** Expressive writing benefits from turning inward. Before you write, close your eyes, take a full, deep inhale/exhale breath, and let go of tension in your body and mind. Repeat a few more times. Let your mind gather itself around the area you'd like to explore.

3. **Date every entry.** If there was a "rule," it would probably be this one. Dating every entry allows you to construct a chronological narrative. It also lets you hear the silence between your entries.

4. **Reread and reflect.** Reread each entry and give yourself a sentence or two of reflection: *As I read this, I am aware of . . .* or *I notice that . . .* or *I'm surprised by . . .* or *I feel/think/want . . .* This reflection synthesizes expression and intuitive understanding.

5. **Write quickly.** You can outsmart writer's block by writing so fast that the Inner Critic and the Inner Editor can't keep pace.

6. **Start writing; keep writing.** Once you begin to write, keep the pen moving. You can edit and fix glitches later if you choose, although editing your journal is never necessary.

7. **Tell the truth as you know it**. Writing it down doesn't make it "real." It does make it noted and acknowledged. When you tell the truth as you

know and experience it, you make room to challenge your assumptions, acknowledge your current reality, release secrecy, and change your mind, heart, and behaviors.

8. **Write naturally.** Do what works for you. If you're more comfortable keyboarding than writing by hand, that's fine. If you want to write in bullet points or poetry, do it. If you "mess up" a pretty hardbound book with scratch-outs and scribbles, so what? Make a collage over the mess. Stay open to your own inner wisdom and intuition, and follow your own internal guidance.

2

The Flourishing Principle

The Principle of Flourishing

The work of being a school principal is a blend of nonstop demands, heart-opening connections, near-constant stress, passionate commitment, and a merry jumble of projects that flop, fizzle, or flourish.

It's easy to get absorbed in the day-to-day demands and the underlying rhythms of the school year. It's easy to forget that the principal's own health and harmony are among the things that need attention. In this chapter, we'll look at eight principles of flourishing, eight ways that principals can rejuvenate and restore balance to the role of steering the ship of a school.

Here are the eight principles of flourishing:

- **Core Values.** Awareness of, connection to, and actions in alignment with the internal compasses that guide you.
- **Balance.** Seeking, finding, and sustaining healthy habits at work, at home, and for yourself.
- **Realism.** Recognizing and acknowledging both facts and feelings; having a grounded sense of "current reality"—the truth about how things are right now.

- **Intention.** The ability to discern what you really want and commit to its actualization.
- **Creativity.** The tangible expression (art, craft, skill) of the innate desire to make things out of the power of inspiration. Also, the innate force that drives "current reality" steadily in the direction of intention through expansive, generative, exploratory choices and actions.
- **Communication.** The ability to initiate dialogue and to listen, discern, and respond, both with others and with yourself.
- **Self-Care.** Knowing what you need and incorporating it into your lifestyle.
- **Wisdom.** Personal awareness of and ability to call on guiding principles, such as (among others) love, gratitude, forgiveness, joy, and grace. For many people, this encompasses a spiritual or faith-based approach to living.

The Flourishing Zone: Gateway to Well-Being

One key to flourishing is ready access to a mental/emotional state that reliably centers, grounds, and sustains you. We'll call it the *flourishing zone.* A reliable method to get into the "zone" comes from the work of Herbert Benson (1976). Here are the steps for his relaxation response, adapted for the flourishing process:

- Choose a quality that represents the sort of well-being you'd like to experience (*clarity, inspiration, peace, loving kindness*) and find a word or image that represents it.
- Take deep breaths while relaxing your body.
- Then place your awareness on the quality you have chosen and the word or image that represents it. Allow thoughts, feelings, images, and ideas to come and go.
- If distracting thoughts or images enter your awareness and pull at you, *passively disregard them* and return your focus to your chosen quality.
- Continue this for as long as you please. Start with a minute or two.
- When you are ready, transition back to a normal state of consciousness through deep breathing, flexing, and stretching.

With practice, your body and mind can integrate the associations so that simply thinking about or bringing to mind the image or feeling of your focus while taking three deep breaths can create a flourishing zone—calm, capable, and clear.

Warm-Ups for the Flourishing Principle

I thrive when . . .

I don't thrive when . . .

from Rosemary's journal

I thrive when:

- *Everyone in the program has children at the center of their thinking.*
- *I get a pat on the back from my supervisor.*
- *A parent stops by unexpectedly with an almond latte and a smile.*
- *Tasks get finished on time or even ahead of schedule.*
- *A walk around the school shows children working hard and learning.*
- *I learn something new and can demonstrate mastery.*
- *A staff member comes to me for advice and leaves with a new idea or thought.*
- *I see a lesson that targets children at the right level and yet has room for differentiation.*
- *A teacher stops in to say thanks for attending a parent/teacher conference and resolving a difficult conflict.*

I don't thrive when:

- *A staff member is thinking of her/his own needs and pushing her/his own agenda.*
- *A parent tells me that she is tired of hearing the word "equity."*
- *I keep working late and feel depleted.*
- *The learning curve is so steep that I feel I'll never catch up.*
- *A staff meeting deteriorates into conflict, staff takes sides, and resolution is not immediately foreseeable.*
- *I pass by a doorway and a teacher is using a caustic tone of voice.*
- *School climate scores don't show improvement in areas we've been targeting.*
- *I go out with my family and focus on the difficult meeting coming up rather than enjoying time together.*

#01. Who Am I?

A character sketch is a description of yourself or someone else. It often starts with physical appearance and moves on to interior qualities: personality characteristics, motivations, fears and prides, essential features, and the state of well-being at the levels of mind/body/heart/spirit.

Start by writing a character sketch (seven to ten minutes) of your "principal self," in the third person, as if you were a compassionate, candid observer. Then write a second character sketch (another seven to ten minutes) from the perspective of someone who knows you—a family member, a faculty or staff member, or a student. When you have completed these, read both and reflect: What stands out for you? What do you notice?

from Rosemary's journal

(Third person about myself) *She stands behind the desk, gazing thoughtfully at the calendar. She has graying hair in a short cut and dark brown eyes. She looks tired, and the calendar is full. She is thinking of what to prioritize and work on for the next precious hour.*

She enjoys problem solving and likes to think of multiple solutions to problems. Writing reports, goals, and summaries is not hard, and she develops a sense of accomplishment with these tasks. Visiting classrooms, when she can connect with teachers, staff, and students, is her favorite part of the day. In the office she is cheerful and positive, yet when the day is over she feels challenged, overwhelmed, and often exhausted.

In her heart, she works for equity for all her students and has strong ideas about education based on her years of experience. She operates from a set of core beliefs. Because these beliefs are questioned daily, her heart is developing tiny cracks in unseen places.

(From the perspective of a second-grade student) *Our principal is really nice. She comes in our classroom and asks us what we are doing. I like to explain to her what we are working on. She knows most of our names and makes jokes. Some of them are funny! She helped me once when this kid in the other class was teasing me, and now she checks in and asks me how things are going. I am* *glad to tell her things are better. I think she makes our school a good place, as she is always around and knows what's going on. She has my friend's artwork hanging in her office, and my other friend said the principal helped her when her parents got a divorce and things got hard at home. She comes to our events and introduced our choir concert. In the morning I see her when my mom drops me off, and I see her at lunchtime. I'm glad we have a principal that I know.*

Reflection: *I loved doing this! The student perspective made me realize that I have more impact on students than I sometimes see, and I am glad I do really know all the students. The self-description helped me also see that I'm doing the best I can in an environment where not everyone has the same end goal, and that helps me persevere. There are so many aspects to my job that are seen by different stakeholders—the teachers, the staff, the parents, the children, and my colleagues at the administration level. It's good to recognize my different roles and to keep my focus on the children.*

#02. The Flourishing Circle

As we begin, let's take inventory of where you are thriving and where you could use some attention.

Figure 2.1 is a Flourishing Circle with eight components to a well-balanced, flourishing life and work life. For each component, circle the number (1 low, 9 high) that represents your present satisfaction with this area of your life. "Satisfaction" can generally be described as the ease with which this quality is incorporated into your day-to-day life, both professional and personal. Use these criteria as a starting place:

- **Core Values.** Your internal compass, pointing to True North.
- **Balance.** Sustaining healthy habits at work, home, with others, and with self.
- **Realism.** Realistic acceptance of "what is" without undue need to deny, rationalize, or avoid.
- **Intention.** The ability to visualize and commit to a desired outcome.
- **Creativity.** The innate drive to express; also, the tangible expression of intention.
- **Communication.** The ability to listen, discern, and respond, to self and others.
- **Self-Care.** Knowing what you need and making sure you have it.
- **Wisdom.** Personal awareness of guiding principles that undergird all else.

When you are finished, review the Flourishing Circle and jot some notes about the individual areas. In which areas do you feel wilted? What would help you flourish? Which areas are flourishing? What's working in these areas?

from Rosemary's journal

Core Values. *This is the aspect of the wheel that jumps out at me first. This was a huge part of our principal learning in "principal school," and we did a lot of work developing these values. I used my top three as a part of my interviews as a solid framework, and when times get tough, they really help me stay focused.*

Balance. *Balance . . . where is it? I've been so busy learning this job, finishing tasks, going to meetings both scheduled and unscheduled that I've lost sight of any balance whatsoever. It's all about the work. I eat, sleep, and dream about* *school. I get up and check emails, I eat lunch and balance the budget, and I get home and rewrite the report. I need to work on this area to be my best, as I will not flourish without balance.*

Realism. *I think realism is sometimes a struggle. Sometimes what I would envision is different from what is actually possible. Not everyone shares my intention, and some people don't agree with my intention. At times, my core values don't seem to match the current reality. When I get together with other principals, I realize we all have this feeling, and then I'm reassured. I need to keep checking into the current reality to match that up with my vision.*

Intention. *I feel pretty solid in the area of intention. My vision is a school where children thrive, and my intention is to do what is best for children. That is the basis of my decisions. I also have an intention that I will always do my best, and that always seems to end up feeling good as a grounding tool.*

Creativity. *At times in this work, I do feel creative. If I'm planning a staff development day, I like to start with something fun and something that builds community and inclusion in the group. I also like to be creative in my problem-solving thinking. What are some other ways to get to the answer? What would help this teacher the most? What does this child need? Creativity seems to come from the heart, and that inspires me.*

Communication. *Communication is an area that I thought was a strength, yet I learn everyday that this is such a critical skill and requires focus. How you craft sentences and responses and requests is SO important. A single word can change meaning and can be interpreted in many ways. In this technological environment, we rely more on emails and less on real, interpersonal communication. I need to remember to also listen carefully as a part of communicating. I learn more in this area than in most others!*

Self-Care. *Self care is "okay." I feel as if I eat well, and I get up early to work out three days a week. If I could, I'd go to a yoga class more often to work on mindfulness, and I'd love to meditate more. Overall, I've been pretty healthy. I do feel tired by Friday! This job really has the expectation that you care for others and are an example of positive thinking and positive energy to others.*

Wisdom. *I have a lot of wisdom to offer. I think I feel this more some days and in certain realms more than in others. I certainly have the teaching experience, curriculum background, and assessment knowledge. When I get together with experienced principals, I realize I came to this job rather late. I taught for a long time, and yes, I was a leader in many areas, but the skill set of the principalship is different from teaching. I'd like to build up my skill levels in administration and keep accessing the wisdom I have to offer.*

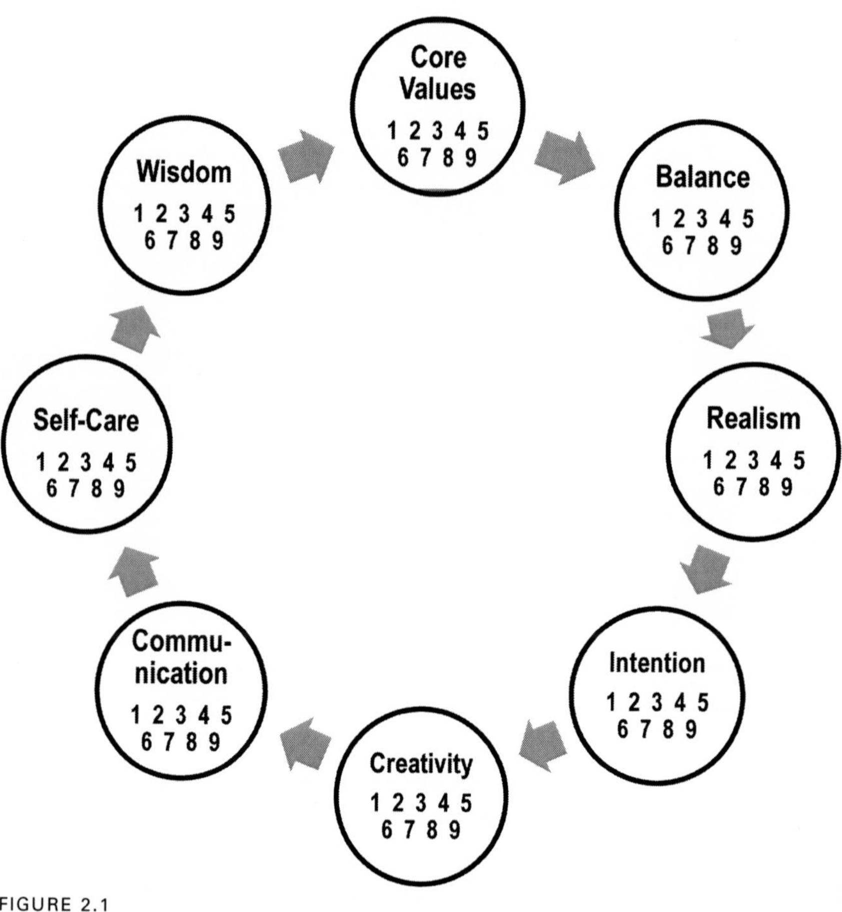

FIGURE 2.1
Flourishing Circle

Notes on the Flourishing Circle

Core Values

Balance

Realism

Intention

Creativity

Communication

Self-Care

Wisdom

#03. Finding the Flourishing Zone

This chapter's introduction includes guidelines for a simple, short meditation that leads you to a place we'll call the *flourishing zone.* Choose a quality, and then choose either the quality word itself (e.g., *peace*) or an image inspired by the quality (e.g., *floating on calm water*). Close your eyes, take some deep breaths, and focus on the quality. Just hold it in your mind. If other thoughts intrude, passively disregard them and return your focus to the quality. Stay there for as long as you like, or for the length of at least several deep, calming breaths.

When you bring yourself back to normal consciousness, make notes. What was the word or image that you chose? What did you experience when you passively disregarded distractions or intrusions? Did insight or awareness come to you as you placed your focus on your centering quality? Did you find the flourishing zone? What was it like? Write for five to ten minutes.

from Rosemary's journal

I really sank into *the meditation. This would be a good practice for me to embrace. I chose the word* clarity, *and what came to mind for me was a compass, which I envision pointing the way to my North Star. My North Star is what is most important to me about my work . . . the children. This relates to my core values that guide me and that bring focus to my thinking.*

As I meditated further, I settled into clarity and how it relates to all aspects of the Flourishing Circle. What is clear? What is the truth? How can I listen and communicate with clarity? How can I share my vision for the school with clarity? A clear and solid compass can guide you through the detours and byways of the day, keep you on your path, and keep you moving forward.

Reflections

Reread what you have written in this session, and write a reflection piece. What do you notice as you read this? Any surprises? Did you have any physical or visceral responses? Any moments of "aha" or insight? Your reflection might begin: *As I read this, I notice . . .* or *As I read this, I am aware of . . .* or *I'm surprised by . . .* or *I understand . . .*

from Rosemary's journal

I notice that this journaling work *is helping me feel successful. I do good work in the classrooms, with children, with teachers and staff, and I need to not be so hard on myself. It was surprising to write a character sketch about myself from a different perspective.*

I also need to bring some balance to my life. It is becoming clear that if I add balance, I'll have more energy and will get more pleasure from the work. Thinking about flourishing is giving me a positive focus.

3

Core Values

Identifying Core Values

Your individual prescription for wellness draws from your *primary* or *core* values—the qualities and characteristics that give your life meaning and purpose.

Some core values are intrinsic. They are imbedded in your personality, as much a part of you as your natural talents or your tendency toward introversion or extraversion. These core values have been with you since birth, and they will naturally surface in childhood or adolescence.

Other core values are acquired through modeling and shaping in families, schools, religious environments, and other early influences. Most schools have vision or mission statements; the core values of the school are often imbedded in these guiding principles.

If you can answer "yes" to the following questions, you are likely dealing with your own core values:

- *If I cannot find or express this quality in a given situation, do I feel dissatisfied, unfulfilled, deprived, unhappy, shut down, unlike myself, or out of sorts? Does it push my crumple button?*

- *Alternatively, when I am able to express this quality, do I come alive? Do I feel satisfied, fulfilled, in alignment with myself, at peace, strong, or in right relationship with myself and others? Do I thrive?*
- *Has this value been with me as far back as I can remember, even if I was unable to fully express it until later in life?*

Hold these curious questions as you move through this chapter.

Warm-Ups on Core Values

I passionately care about . . .

An injustice that makes me really angry is . . .

from Rosemary's journal

I passionately care about *all people being treated with dignity. I cringe inside when I hear anyone mistreating a child, being sarcastic, or belittling a child. I also feel the same with racial jokes or slurs, and I take a stand against these comments. Even if the comments are just thoughtless or perhaps made in some ignorance, I don't think they can be overlooked. What we say affects others, and our words and thoughts have a ripple effect.*

An injustice that makes me really angry is *any type of mistreatment. I'm not sure where this deep feeling comes from. It's why I became a vegetarian years ago, and maybe why I went into teaching, so that in some small part of the universe I can create and maintain what I hope is a safe, supportive learning environment.*

#04. Naming Values

Go through the list of values in Table 3.1 and circle all that resonate with you. Which qualities are essential to flourishing? When you are complete, go through the list again and narrow it down to ten core values that have been with you all your life, even when you couldn't fully express them. Include any that you can't fully express now. If you need to add words to the list, do so. Write out your list of ten core values.

As principal, it is likely that your core values will intersect with the core values of your school. If your school hasn't formally defined or articulated its core values, you may want to separately complete this process for the school.

from Rosemary's journal

01. Honesty
02. Humor
03. Balance
04. Equity
05. Safety
06. Compassion
07. Responsibility
08. Consistency
09. Respect
10. Integrity

Table 3.1. List of Values

Acceptance	Forgiveness	Nonconformity	Spirituality
Accountability	Freedom	Nonjudgment	Status
Achievement	Friendship	Nurturing	Stewardship
Acknowledgment	Generativity	Obedience	Strength
Adventure	Generosity	Organization	Status
Appreciation	Grace	Ownership	Success
Authenticity	Gratitude	Partnership	Support
Balance	Harmony	Passion	Synergy
Benevolence	Health	Peace	Technology
Building	Helping others	Play	Time for self
Caring	Honesty	Power	Time mgmt
Challenge	Honor	Prestige	Togetherness
Change/variety	Humor	Productivity	Touch
Communication	Inclusion	Progressive	Tradition
Community	Independence	Prosperity	Trail-blazing
Compassion	Influencing	Purity	Truth
Competence	Inspiration	Reflection	Unity
Connection	Interdependence	Religion	Validation
Consistency	Integrity	Renewal	Vision
Courage	Intimacy	Research	Vitality
Creativity	Joy	Respect	Wealth
Curiosity	Justice	Responsibility	Wellness
Decisiveness	Kindness	Rights	Wholeness
Diversity	Knowledge	Risk-taking	Wisdom
Duty	Leadership	Rules	Work
Eficiency	Love	Safety	Worth
Empathy	Loyalty	Security	
Empowerment	Management	Self-actualization	Add others:
Ethics	Mastery	Self-respect	____________
Equality	Meaningful work	Serenity	____________
Equity	Mediation	Simplicity	____________
Faith	Mission	Sincerity	____________
Fame	Motivation	Status	____________
Family	Mutuality	Stewardship	____________
Fidelity	Nature	Social activism	____________

#05. Defining Values

Write definitions for each of your core values—personalized, concrete, specific articulations that describe your own sense of right relationship with each value. These can be factual, objective definitions (such as the definitions for the aspects of the flourishing principle in Figure 2.1), or they may be more metaphoric, as Rosemary's are.

from Rosemary's journal

Honesty *is a gentleman. He speaks the truth and yet knows when to hold back for the sake of honor. He is transparent with his words and never has to hide.*

Humor *is like Mercury, darting in on silvery winged feet to gently send the message "lighten up."*

Balance *is a rock planted firmly in the ground. All sides get a turn in the bright light of the sun. The rock won't shift or sway. It is solidly anchored.*

Equity *is the torch of the Statue of Liberty, shining and beckoning to welcome everyone to the room, regardless of race, creed, or color.*

Safety *is the Iron Man of the school, protecting all who enter the grounds with care and attention to detail. No corner, edge, or protrusion is overlooked.*

Compassion *is a gray-cloaked nurse making the rounds. Her cool, deft hand makes sure all are taken care of.*

Responsibility *is an invisible cloak that settles on my shoulders, looking like linen and feeling like chain mail. It can never be shed and weighs me down.*

Consistency *is calm and collected. He treats everyone with a sense of fairness, follows protocols and rules, and yet knows when to bend them for the good of all. Behind his back, people admire him.*

Respect *is a gold-plated mirror reflecting back to us how to treat others. He has a sense of formality. "See who I am? Treat me authentically and value me."*

Integrity *is a soldier, standing tall and hiding behind no one. He steps up front and reports for duty.*

#06. Making Art from a Core Value

For this exercise you will need basic collage supplies: old magazines (calendars, newspapers, newsletters, even junk mail), a glue stick, scissors, plus any other art supplies you might want on hand.

Choose one of your core values, perhaps one that seems elusive or distant at the present time. Practice the flourishing zone meditation, using your chosen value as the focus word. When you return to normal consciousness, page through the magazines and cut out images and words that reflect or symbolize the core value. Arrange the images and words on a journal page, a large piece of poster board, a 3x5 index card, or a plain piece of paper. Embellish the images with your own art if you choose. When you're finished, write about the collage. What is the overall statement the collage makes? What do the images represent? What is your internal response when you look at it?

from Rosemary's journal

I can see that my inner artist *is longing for some release. Collaging was a right-brain activity that my left-brain-immersed self enjoyed totally! I chose integrity. Some beautiful images jumped out at me as I thumbed through old magazines. Collaging was fun, as the images were there, I just got to arrange them into a meaningful picture, and I was pleased with the final result.*

I stayed small, and worked on a 5x8 card as a background. The main image is a veteran, saluting, in black and white. This conveys my "soldier" image, integrity being "front and center" and ready for duty. In the background are several images, all meaningful to me. Upper left, another soldier image is embossed on a coin; perhaps he is a crusader. Upper right, a Native American warrior; again, the warrior ready to do battle against injustice. Middle left, a mother holding her child, perhaps guarding and protecting. Lower left, a lion in profile from an ancient brick wall, walking proudly with teeth bared. Finally, lower right, a guardian angel image, surprisingly with Michael Jackson enrobed with gorgeous angel wings. The whole, greater than the sum of its parts, speaks to me, and I've put the finished collage on my desk.

#07. Values-Based Problem Solving

Now let's put your core values to work! Think about a difficult or troubling situation at work, and describe it briefly. Choose three core values from your list. First, write a concise summary of the difficult situation. Then apply your first value to the situation. What might happen if you were to perceive the situation through the lens of this value? What might shift? What might you see differently? What new possibilities might surface? Write your responses. If you wish, repeat with the second and third values.

from Rosemary's journal

If I applied my core value of consistency *to the situation of the front office, there would be more spaciousness and openness. Managing an office is not an easy skill to learn, and if things aren't moving smoothly out there, it's hard for things to go smoothly in my office. I need to meet consistently with my assistant. One management program for principals recommends daily meetings. So we'll start that in the mornings. We can look at the day coming up, plan ahead, and troubleshoot. I should also have consistent check-ins with other office people and with the nurse's office. I need to set some protocols around posting notices in the office. One went up on the refrigerator last week that wasn't too friendly, and those need to be run by me before going up. I'd also like to check in with the custodian monthly and do both a custodial checklist and a safety checklist. These consistencies—large and small—will help!*

Reflections

Reflect on your core values. What do you notice? Any "aha" moments? What surprises you? Is there anything you see or understand differently?

from Rosemary's journal

My core values, *like the lion image in my collage, sometimes remain dormant and calm. Yet if an issue comes up that touches on them, I will bare my teeth and raise my hackles. I am surprised at times by the strength I have in these areas. I feel like these values keep me strong and aligned with my truth. Listing them, journaling about them, and giving them attention has been a renewal of what is important to me.*

4

Balance

Cultivating Balance

When you are optimally balanced in an area of life, it may not be ideal or perfect, but you are content with what life has offered you in this area. You know you are doing the best you can to maintain or improve your quality of life.

On the other hand, if you are out of balance in an area, it may evoke feelings such as restlessness, unhappiness, stress, dissatisfaction, frustration, resentment, hopelessness, anger, fear, or anxiety—and all the behaviors associated with those feelings.

In this chapter, you'll learn to use the Balance Wheel (Figure 4.1), a way to quickly get a visual picture of the current state of balance, or imbalance, in major aspects of your life.

Check in with the Balance Wheel quarterly. You'll likely be surprised at your progress!

Warm-Ups for Balance

I know I'm out of balance when I . . .

To stay in balance, I wish I would remember . . .

from Rosemary's journal

I know I'm out of balance when I *sense that all is not right with my inner alignment. Sometimes I'm not sure what exactly is not balanced, I just have the sense of something missing. I generally think of myself as well rounded and somewhat fulfilled, yet that sense of incompleteness can haunt me. I need to look for what is missing.*

To stay in balance I wish I would remember *that "moderation in all things" is such a good guide. I tend to get too pulled into what I'm doing at work. I lose sight of the bigger whole that is my total self. I take the responsibility of running the school so seriously that it weighs heavily on me. I tend to take the role of the responsible one. My friends tease me about not being a risk taker. Lack of balance holds me back.*

#08. The Balance Wheel

Figure 4.1 is the Balance Wheel. Assume that the center for each wedge on the Balance Wheel represents the complete absence of satisfaction/balance, and the outer rim represents a fullness of balance and satisfaction.

With a pen, pencil, crayon, colored pencil, or marker, color your satisfaction with each of the life areas. Your full satisfaction would be represented by a space colored to the outer edge. Partial satisfaction would be indicated proportionately. Dissatisfaction would be indicated by a small colored wedge near the center of the circle. Remember that this is *your* satisfaction you are measuring, not the "norm" or expectation of others. When you are complete, write a sentence or two that summarizes your state of being in each area.

from Rosemary's journal

Career/work/activity: *My job is very active and busy, yet not totally satisfying, as I lack balance. I give 110 percent here and this causes other spaces on the wheel to be depleted. So, it is maybe one-third full.*

Relationships/love/family: *This is partially full. My husband and children provide support and some balance. They are proud of my work and have seen me work toward my goals. We have strong relationships. The nurturing and sustaining is my responsibility too, and I need to keep effort up in this area.*

Fun/recreation: *This area is suffering! I can go out, for example, to a concert, and not fully enjoy the music as I'm focused on the job, even after hours. I'm barely there at all.*

Emotional health/personal growth: *I colored this pie piece half full. I have grown a lot and learned a lot, yet sometimes the learning curve has been too steep. I am trying to balance the emotional health of not only myself but also, at times, the staff I work with. This leaves me depleted.*

Health/body: *I'm doing pretty well here. I manage to get up and go work out three mornings a week, and I like the routine. Overall, I eat well. I'm healthy. This is colored nearly out to the outer line.*

Home/environment: *This is a fully filled-in area. I enjoy being home, I enjoy the garden, and because now we are empty nesters, the house stays organized. Not that I don't miss the children!*

Finance/security: *Both my husband and I are working and have saved for the future. This is a secure/balanced area.*

Spirituality/religion: *Ouch! This area is basically empty. I feel like this lack of inner work is going to affect me in the long run. Some of the group work I've done helps here, but overall, I need to give this some focus . . . how?*

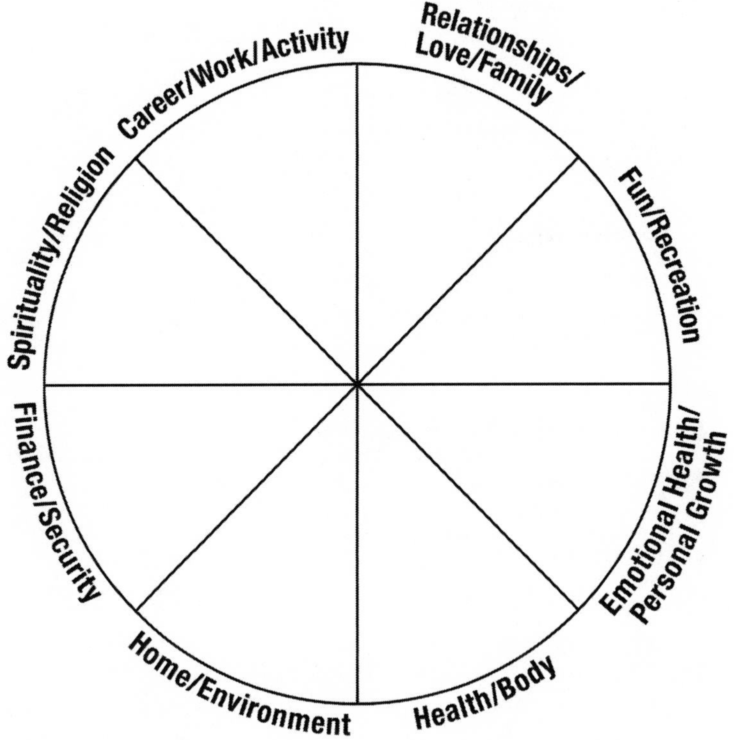
Career/Work/Activity
Relationships/
Love/Family
Fun/Recreation
Emotional Health/
Personal Growth
Health/Body
Home/Environment
Finance/Security
Spirituality/Religion

FIGURE 4.1

#09. Balance Inventory

Beginning with the wedges that have the most white space (representing the least balance or satisfaction), take your own inventory. Begin by naming the area of life balance, and include the following:

- Where am I now?
- Where do I want to be for optimum balance?
- What are three action steps I could take to get there?
- What is one action step I can take, starting now, to move toward greater balance?

Career/Work

Where am I now? *Overwhelmed, no limits or boundaries around time on the job, feeling like I have to get it all done and done well.*

Where do I want to be for optimum balance? *Some down time, some ability to enjoy life and what it can offer me, and not feeling like the dictionary definition of "workaholic."*

What are three action steps I could take to get there?

1. *Set aside Sundays as a day off, and use the day to rejuvenate and refresh myself.*
2. *Stop working at 5:30 p.m. every day. Clean up and be out the door by 6:00 p.m. Write notes for the morning so my brain can let go and switch gears.*
3. *Don't look at emails or computer notes in the evening. Keep boundaries clear between work and school.*

What is one action step I can take, starting now, to move toward greater balance? *I will work on all three, as they all focus on boundaries between work and home. Starting immediately, I will not read emails once I get home.*

#10. Core Values and the Balance Wheel

How might your core values support your efforts to seek and find more balance in your life? Compare your list of core values to your balance inventories. Which of your core values might help you take the action steps needed to come into balance? What might the possibilities be? Jot one or more values in the white spaces of your balance wheel. Then, for each area, write: *If I applied my core value of _______ to this situation, then . . .*

from Rosemary's journal

If I applied my core value of compassion *to myself, then I might feel some melting. I wrote this on the spirituality wedge. Compassion wells up deep within me for others. Where is it for myself? I get angry, uptight, and critical of myself. The compassion needs to start within and build from there. I can take some time each day to feel that warmth and allow it to move toward my inner critic, smoothing out the critical side and strengthening my self-confident side.*

Reflections

Read what you have written about balance. What do you notice? What have you become aware of? Are there shifts or changes you can make that will help you bring balance to your life?

from Rosemary's journal

It felt strange *to look at all parts of myself on the balance wheel and see which parts are fulfilled and which are neglected. I could visually see what my life has and what it lacks. How revealing this was, and in some ways it was intimidating. I am not as well rounded as I thought. I notice questions arising. Some are back to being critical: How did I ignore my spiritual self for so long? Some are guiding: How can I build up this part of the wheel? How can I let go of some of the weights that are holding me down? How can I let some lightness in and let go of some heaviness? It's all good. Already I feel more balanced, although there's a lot of work to do.*

5

Realism

Telling Yourself the Truth

The capacity to be realistic—to tell ourselves the truth about what is actually happening—is a great asset in the quest for balance at work, home, and life. While it might seem self-evident that responsible adults would be realistic and tell themselves and others the truth, most of us slip up on this in ways that may not be immediately apparent.

Let's say you've got an innovative idea for restructuring a part of the school that everyone agrees needs fixing. What you're thinking about has never been tried before, and although it isn't actually risky, it's edgy and original. It would require buy-in from others who don't usually think outside the box.

As soon as you start actually thinking about writing up your ideas, an inner voice roars to life: *Are you nuts?* or *Nobody will go for that!* or *Who do you think you are?* or *You can't do that!*

The late cognitive-behavioral psychologist Dr. Albert Ellis called this our *stinkin' thinkin'*, also known as *irrational beliefs* (1997). Irrational beliefs express as the self-talk that jumps to conclusions based on experiences, judgments, messages, internalized beliefs, and habituated behaviors. Much of the time these beliefs have little or no basis in actual reality and can be successfully challenged with more realistic statements: *No, I'm not*, or *Some won't go for it, but some will*, or *I think I am an innovative, resourceful principal*, or *Yes, I can, if I decide it's the right thing to do.*

Robert Fritz, a pioneer in structural dynamics, emphasizes the importance of an intimate relationship with *current reality*. He recommends developing the capacity to acknowledge, simply and nonjudgmentally, what is "real" about the current moment, situation, or experience. This includes objective, dispassionate, accurate naming of thoughts, feelings, beliefs, behaviors, and circumstances with regard to your situation (Fritz 1989).

Current reality in the case of your new idea might include excitement, a creative burst, apprehension about how it might be received, insecurity about being made fun of, uncertainty about whether or not it would be worth the time investment to develop the idea, an inner sense that the idea might actually work well, *and* those nattering voices telling you that you're nuts and you don't know what you're doing. In other words, those voices are part—but not all—of the whole savory stew of your current reality.

In this chapter, you'll learn quick writing methods to tell yourself the truth. We'll counter "stinkin' thinkin'," confront irrational beliefs, and accurately describe current reality. You'll learn a handy tip for keeping your truth in the foreground. Here we go!

Warm-Ups for Realism

My irrational thoughts/beliefs . . .

My current reality . . .

I tell myself the truth about . . .

from Rosemary's journal

My irrational thoughts/beliefs *can sometimes be overwhelming. I have a pretty strong inner critic that I have to work on at times. It helps when I remember to "lock it in the closet," as a wise friend advised! I can let myself go down several paths of insecurity and uncertainty. I judge myself for worrying that I can't solve every conflict with a good outcome. One of my irrational beliefs is that "everyone" will be upset if I don't collect "everyone's" input on every decision. Yet that's clearly not possible, and it's often not necessary or even desirable.*

My current reality *is that I have multiple viewpoints and a multitude of experience in education. I have conflict-resolution skills. I was an award-winning teacher. As a teacher I chaired many committees both at the building level and at the district level, and I trained other teachers in literacy. My current reality is also truly that some of this previous work did not prepare me adequately for all the challenges of the principalship. So there's always more to learn.*

#11. Transforming "Stinkin' Thinkin'"

Bring to mind a current situation at work that has activated your negative self-talk. Describe it briefly. Then listen carefully to your negative self-talk about the situation. Divide a piece of paper into two columns. On the left, write the self-talk you hear. On the right, challenge each statement and reframe it as a more realistic, accurate statement. Here's an example:

Situation: I have an idea to solve a problem at school, but it's pretty out-of-the-box.

Irrational beliefs	Rational reframes
Are you nuts?	No, I am not nuts.
Nobody will go for that!	Sure, some won't go for it, but (names) probably will.
Who do you think you are?	I think I am an innovative, resourceful principal.
You can't do that!	I can do it, if it's the right thing to do, and others agree.

When you are complete, write for five to ten minutes about the situation, having moved some "stinkin' thinkin'" to the sidelines. When you're done, reread and reflect on the ease or difficulty of moving beyond negative self-talk. Also reflect on any new possibilities or perspectives.

from Rosemary's journal

I want to take on the growing problem *of faculty time being eaten up, often unproductively, in sitting on too many committees and having too many meetings. Union rules are becoming clearer that teachers are only obligated to attend a limited number of meetings a month. Many committees were set up years ago and are outdated or redundant. Also, some committee jobs carry a lot more weight than others—some are leadership roles, some are decision-making roles, and some are "attending" roles. I want to streamline and combine some committees. Then I want to weight the committee activities with points and make it equitable—those who are in leadership or decision making earn more points than those who have "attending" roles, and full-time teachers will need about twice as many points as half-time teachers.*

Situation: Making faculty committee assignments more equitable.	
Irrational beliefs	**Rational reframes**
Everyone will hate this idea.	*Some teachers will be unhappy, but quite a few will feel relieved and heard.*
Some of these committees are "sacred cows"—change will be impossible.	*Change can and does happen!* *We're always changing something at our school.*
We don't have time to do this.	*It's hard to find time for change, but it will actually save time in the long run.*
There will be so much resistance!	*There is always resistance, and there are always ways to manage resistance through communication and collaboration.*

Reflection: *This sounds like it could work. It's all in the planning and presentation. I can begin by surveying teachers and staff to get their feedback on which committees are essential and which can be combined or eliminated. Then, when we have that information in place, we can begin to work on restructuring. This might not be as challenging as I thought!*

#12. Reality Cards

For this process, you'll need some 3 × 5 index cards. Every time you reframe an irrational belief into a realistic statement, write it on a card. Begin to build a deck of cards that hold the new realities that create different thought patterns. In addition to your own reframed, affirmative beliefs, you can also include inspirational quotations, lines of poetry, Bible verses or quotes from other sacred texts, or other spiritual principles—anything that represents truth to you. Rosemary illustrates her reality cards with doodles, sketches, and swooshes of watercolor.

Carry the deck with you and leaf through it during odd moments throughout the day. Use one card as a focal point as you practice your flourishing zone meditations, or keep a few on your desk for quick, deep-breath reality checks!

Write down ten or more quotes, thoughts, inspirations, lines, or/and verses that would make good reality cards. Then transfer them to 3 × 5 cards.

from Rosemary's journal

Change can happen. —Rosemary

Parents support teachers and value their time. —Rosemary

I am not afraid of storms, for I am learning how to sail my ship. —Louisa May Alcott

Out beyond ideas of wrongdoing and rightdoing, there is a field. I'll meet you there. —Rumi

The best thing for being sad . . . is to learn something. —T. H. White

i thank You God for most this amazing day. —e. e. cummings

"You're Number 1!" —my first student teacher; this became a catchphrase for each other.

"I've got your back." —from a principal friend; this, too, became a regular catchphrase.

"Kids are worth it!" —my friend Barbara

"Leave dignity intact." —my friend Barbara

#13. The ABCs

Albert Ellis's model of rational-emotive behavior therapy (REBT) (1997) offers the simple but highly effective idea that it is not an *event* that causes us to feel terrible, it is the *meaning or belief we ascribe to the event*, which is usually irrational. In other words—our "stinkin' thinkin'" gets us in trouble by exaggerating, catastrophizing, jumping to conclusions, or distorting truth in other ways. As an old proverb states, we take a button and sew a coat onto it.

In this model, we assume that *rational* thoughts or ideas are ones that are measurable, actual, factual, data based, real, observable. *Irrational* thoughts or ideas have no rational evidence to support them. There is often rational evidence that disproves them.

The format looks like this:

A = **Activating Event**. Describe the situation that caused the negative feeling or self-talk.

B = **Belief**. List the *belief* or *self-talk* you told yourself about A.

C = **Consequence**. The negative feeling that resulted—confusion, doubt, shame, unworthiness, and more—from your self-talk in B.

D = **Disputing**. This comes in two parts:

> D1: Is there any rational (real, evidence based, actual, factual) evidence to support the truth of B? (Hint: If this is truly an irrational thought, the answer will likely be NO.)
>
> D2: What is the belief or self-talk about "A" that is more rational, real, actual, and factual? Write it down.

E = **Effective New Emotion**. What is the emotional response that arises as an outcome of telling yourself a more rational belief (D2)?

Using the ABCs Worksheet at Figure 5.1 and Rosemary's example, take a recent upsetting situation and work yourself through to a more rational thought and a more effective emotion.

from Rosemary's journal

A = Activating Event. *As a first-year principal, I misallocated funds and mistakenly credited designated funds to my general fund. This made my budget work out well! I was very proud of myself. Then my huge error was discovered.*

B = Belief (negative self-talk).*"You obviously don't know what you're doing! You made a stupid mistake. How could you? Now everyone will think you're stupid or careless! This is a disaster."*

C = Consequence (negative emotions). *I felt ignorant, bad at math, incompetent, inexperienced, mad at myself.*

D = Disputing.

D1 (Rational evidence to support?) *No.*

D2 (More rational self-talk)

It's true that I'm still in a first-year learning curve, but I do know what I'm doing. I made an honest mistake. I'm good at budgeting, math, and problem solving. This is inconvenient and even embarrassing, but it's not a disaster. I'll get it fixed, and it will be fine.

E = Effective New Emotion. *Relief, embarrassment, determination.*

ABCs Worksheet

A = Activating Event. Briefly describe the upsetting situation. What happened?

B = Belief. What assumptions or meaning did you make as a result of A? What was your self-talk? What conclusions did you jump to?

C = Consequence. What negative or unwanted feelings arose from A?

D = Disputing.

D1: Is there any rational (real, evidence-based, actual, factual) evidence to support the truth of B? (The answer will likely be NO.)

D2: What is the belief or self-talk about A that is more rational, real, actual and factual?

E = Effective new emotion(s). What is the emotional response that arises as an outcome of telling yourself a more rational, accurate belief?

Adapted from the work of Albert Ellis (1997).

#14. Current Reality

Current reality is a series of accurate, objective, nonjudgmental observations about what's true for you (*reality*) in the present moment (*current*). The list is written in simple, declarative statements or bullet points, stripped of apology, excuse, or defense.

Using a current situation at school—one you've already written about, or a new one—write a bullet-point list about current reality. Remember that everything—shame, excitement, righteous indignation, mistaken belief, desire—are equal and neutral parts of current reality. See if you can get at least seven items on your list.

from Rosemary's journal

Current reality about the budget

- *Budgets are complex mechanisms.*
- *There will always be budgetary constraints.*
- *I am a solid mathematician and can make this balance.*
- *I have time to finish the budget.*
- *My assistant can help me with parts of this.*
- *Starting over is a good way to recheck my work so far.*
- *I'm still a little emotionally rattled by this.*
- *I feel better now that I have a plan.*

Reflections

What have you learned about yourself, your irrational beliefs, current reality, and capacity for realism? Reread your responses and give yourself some feedback.

from Rosemary's journal

Thinking about current reality *can provide a "checks and balance" system. As a principal, I seem to work in a void and often alone. I don't always have someone else saying, "Hey, lighten up." With this strategy, I can be my own check-and-balance. Thinking about, listing, and checking in with current reality can show me where I really am and where I have to go. It can provide an accurate road map for my journey. I learned a lot from this process, both about myself and about the job. I also loved making my reality cards, and I can see how making some "current reality" cards would also help a lot, especially in situations like the budget.*

6

Intention

The Power of Intention

Think of the most visionary leaders you have known. Think about the big dreams they dreamed, the achievements they realized under challenging odds. What makes a visionary's dreams come to life?

Often, it's the power of intention.

Intention is desire infused with muscle. Desires, abstract and uncommitted, are the ideas you have about what you'd like to realize. Intentions are concrete and committed. Intentions are the desires you are willing to bring into being.

When you move a desire into the realm of intention, you make a conscious choice to apply skills, time, talents, resources, energy, attention, perseverance, and commitment to its actualization. Intentions are desires that woke up from the dream, got out of bed, and got to work.

It's helpful to have an active, vivid mental image of what it will look and feel like to enjoy the manifested intention. Some like to externalize the image via sketching, painting, making a collage, or writing a clear description. For others, entering the flourishing zone and focusing on the intention, while passively disregarding intrusive or distracting thoughts, will keep the imagined final outcome in the foreground.

Simply visualizing the outcome of an intention is not enough. Intention without action is illusion. That's a crucial awareness, so let's say it again: *Intention without action is illusion.*

When we hold firmly to the vision of the outcome (intention) and acknowledge our circumstances as they are (current reality), the discrepancy between the two becomes clear. That's when you take action. Any step in the direction of your vision will change current reality and move you closer to actualizing your intention. Even the ones that don't work will advance your movement toward vision (Fritz, 1989), because we must often learn about "no" on the way to "yes." In Rosemary's example of her first-year budget woes, she took steps with the intention to create the vision of a workable budget. One of her steps—allocation of designated funds—didn't work. But even her mistake got her closer to her completed intention, because she learned with certainty how to budget designated funds. Rosemary never made that particular mistake again, so all future budgets were streamlined.

Your intention is a powerful tool for thriving. In this chapter, you'll identify your desires, select some intentions, brainstorm action steps to take, and make an action plan. Then you'll take your next step!

Warm-Ups on Intention

My relationship with intention . . .

When my intention is clear . . .

If I could choose anything . . .

from Rosemary's journal

When my intention is clear, *I am clear. I am definite, I see the way and I see the goal. The path may be bumpy and I may not see every hill and valley along* *the road, but I am clear about the end result, and I have a good feeling as I set out. A clear intention is like a bell ringing a true note.*

If I could choose anything, *it would be to be more at peace with myself and this work. I have such a "caretaking," sensitive side that I have to remind myself often to not take things personally and that I am doing my best. This work goes so deep and involves so many others that there is a constant surrounding and influx of information, personalities, wants, and needs. Peace would bring more inner calmness in the face of the storms.*

#15. What Do I Want?

Make a list of eight to twelve things that you would like to have in your life. These can be large or small, work related or personal, serious or frivolous. Don't limit yourself by what you think is realistic or possible. Limit yourself only by whether or not you actually want this, for yourself or your school, from an interior point of view. If you would derive satisfaction from the outcome, or from the process of creating it, put it on your list. Ask yourself: *If I could have this, would I take it* (Fritz, 1989)*?* If the answer is *yes*, then put it on your list.

from Rosemary's journal

What do I not want? *I'm a person who used to want for very little, who was in a classroom creating a safe, consistent, and generally lively environment. I worked for the good of my class and kids, and I had time for family and for friends. Now I am working for hundreds of children, for a group of parents, for a school board, for a building, and for a diverse staff. I am working under state law, federal law, and school board rules that have to be followed. I want:*

- *a more cohesive staff*
- *a more spacious school with room for small groups to meet*
- *a better playground*
- *a bigger budget*
- *an assistant who understands me and my vision and sees my intentions*
- *an hour a day to work on office tasks so I can go home at a reasonable time*
- *the ability to turn off the school processing that happens in my brain during down time so that I can enjoy outings*
- *a mentor to help me sort out the difficult stuff*
- *someone to plan vacations for me . . . fly here, stay here, travel here . . . with no work on my part*
- *to meet Neil Diamond and perhaps sing backup on one song . . .*

#16. Setting Intention

Get in the flourishing zone by closing your eyes, relaxing, and spending a few minutes focusing on the concept of intention. Passively disregard any intrusive thoughts, and let your mind rest easily. When you return to normal consciousness, review your list. For each of the items that you would take if you could have them, set your intention by writing individual statements: *I intend* . . . Follow with anything else you want to note: why you want it, what it feels like when you imagine having it, what you see when you visualize it. The more detailed and descriptive you can be, the better.

from Rosemary's journal

- **I intend to build** *a more cohesive staff.*
  - *I see a group of people with the common goal of what is best for children.*
  - *I see decision making becoming quicker, easier, and still collaborative.*
  - *I see boundaries dissolving, staff supporting each other, and more sharing of ideas.*
- **I intend to create** *a more spacious school with room for small groups to meet.*
  - *I see creatively reconceptualizing the space we have to get the most out of each room.*
  - *I see surveying the building to see which rooms are empty and when.*
- **I intend to a create** *a better playground.*
  - *I see less playground conflict.*
  - *The task of monitoring children would be easier with clear boundaries.*
  - *I see parents working together to do this project.*
- **I intend to have** *a bigger budget.*
  - *ha!*
- **I intend to train** *an assistant who understands me and my vision and sees my intentions.*
  - *I see us meeting daily, and one day a week I state some of my visions and build cohesion and understanding.*
- **I intend to find** *an hour a day to work on office tasks so I can go home at a reasonable time.*
  - *I feel less tired.*
  - *I can prioritize more.*
  - *I can schedule this into my calendar more and stick to it.*

- **I intend to develop** *the ability to turn off the school processing that happens in my brain during down time so that I can enjoy outings.*
  - *I envision a sort of "traveling home" meditation where I unwind and leave work behind and look forward to some time with my family and friends.*
- **I intend to attract** *a mentor to help me sort out the difficult stuff.*
  - *I will ask someone to be my mentor.*
  - *I will use friends informally as mentors.*
  - *I will ask the district for a formal mentor.*
- **I intend to find** *someone to plan vacations for me . . . fly here, stay here, travel here . . . with no work on my part.*
  - *Try an automotive travel membership for trip ideas.*
  - *Make a list of to-dos.*
  - *Use the Internet.*
  - *Get referrals from friends.*
- **I intend to meet** *Neil Diamond and perhaps sing backup on one song.*
  - *Perhaps Ellen DeGeneres can help me with this one!*
  - *Oh well, some intentions just take longer than others . . .*

#17. One Hundred Action Steps

Guidelines for Lists of 100

- *Write quickly.*
- *Write in staccato words and phrases.*
- *Let yourself repeat.*
- *Write quickly.*
- *Stay with it until the end.*
- *It's OK to repeat.*
- *Finish the list.*
- *You can repeat! It's OK!*

One of the most reliable ways to get below the surface, past the obvious, and find out what's really going on is to write a List of 100. As the name suggests, this is a very long list (one hundred entries) on a predetermined theme. However, the structure of the list is one of staccato words and phrases, so the writing goes very quickly.

If you're following the guidelines, you should be able to write a List of 100 in twenty to twenty-five minutes; it's not a huge time investment. When you let yourself repeat, it's also not difficult or cumbersome (although it admittedly can get briefly tedious). When you're complete, go back through and group your list entries into themes or categories. You might be surprised at the results!

For this exercise, set aside an uninterrupted thirty minutes. Choose one of the intentions that you set, preferably one that already needs action. Write a list of one hundred action steps you could take in the direction of your intention. Write quickly, let yourself repeat, write in staccato words and phrases, keep your pen moving, let yourself repeat, and just keep writing. If you get stuck, write "stuck, stuck" and keep going.

Intention without action is illusion. Take a deep breath and get into action!

from Rosemary's journal

Excerpts from **List of 100 Action Steps for a More Cohesive Staff**

1. *have more time for staff interactions*
2. *start off staff meetings with an inclusive/team-building activity*
3. *build some opening/closure "ceremony" into meetings and workdays*

4. *have different groups meet on different topics*
5. *do some personal sharing*
6. *do some individual/dyad/group work*
7. *more staff interactions at meetings*
8. *build common agreements*
9. *staff interactions—more and better quality*
10. *find ways to include all staff into activities*
11. *delegate to new people, not the same old stuff*
12. *build shared leadership*
13. *continue to have common planning times in schedule*
14. *attend team meetings*
15. *have more engaging staff meetings*

#18. Categorizing Your List

This process will also take about twenty to thirty minutes. When you're finished writing your List of 100, go back through and group your list entries into themes or categories. Assign identifying names to your categories/themes. You'll probably have a *miscellaneous* category for the random entries that don't fit anywhere else. When you're done, add up the numbers in each category.

When you are complete, you will see your preponderance of ideas about taking a next step. What step seems to be organically emerging for you? Or, what step do you want to take next?

from Rosemary's journal

Staff meeting ideas—54 percent

Leadership ideas—27 percent

Staff interactions—9 percent

Hiring—6 percent

Miscellaneous—4 percent

Wow!! More than half *of my ideas about building a more cohesive staff have to do with meetings. I guess this makes sense; meetings are where we most consistently and regularly come together. The current reality, though, is that everyone (even me) dreads meetings because they're so often unproductive and time sucking. But I can harvest this 54 percent to create dynamic, productive, interesting, and even fun meetings so that we can get more done and leave feeling energized and motivated.*

____

____

____

____

____

#19. Taking Your Next Step

Take a step—any step—in the direction of your vision by setting your intention and getting into action. If the step doesn't yield the outcomes you want, that's still good news! Remember that *any step you take with intention in the direction of your vision helps you get there—even the ones that don't work* (Fritz, 1989). Take the step, then make notes here about what worked, what felt easy, what felt challenging, any surprises—and be sure to note how your current reality has changed.

from Rosemary's journal

Since staff meeting ideas *are clearly the dominant theme here, I've decided to immediately implement ideas #2 and #3 from my List of 100 (starting with an inclusive/team-building activity and incorporating opening/closure ceremonies or rituals into meetings). Each will be easy to do and won't take up much time. I attended a workshop recently where the leader handled introductions by tossing a "koosh" ball around the circle and asking each person to say their name and one thing they wanted the group to know about them. It was fun, it went fast, and we had some laughs when the ball got tossed over someone's head or when two people grabbed for it. I will start my next meeting with a koosh ball, asking them for a topic or idea to place on the agenda (or to second or third an item already there). I'll do the first toss, and then I can make notes. This will advance current reality as an inclusive team-building activity, and perhaps it will become a ritualized opening. There's more to do in these areas, of course, but this would be a great start. Exciting!*

Reflections

Reflect on your writes about intention. What possibilities might be opening up for you? How is it to select and declare an intention and plan a first step toward actualizing it?

from Rosemary's journal

These are such varied ideas *and probably the most on one topic I've ever come up with! This will be a great strategy to apply to other areas and to do with staff around brainstorming and problem solving. I enjoyed the sorting, and it was informative to see where ideas sorted themselves out. It seems easiest to think of ideas to use at staff meetings.*

The deep work that is coming to me is to look at the historical elephants in the room. In some ways this is overwhelming and difficult work, and yet I'm not sure we can move forward if we don't shine some lights on the past.

It is frustrating to just have one hour a week for staff meetings. At some schools, staff members get up and leave if principals go over the hour. This is my current reality as a principal—try to accomplish tasks, build a strong team, improve student achievement, and yet have limited time and resources and buy-in.

In summary, I think we will make the greatest progress as a group if we identify old issues, see where we can reach some resolution, and then move forward. And I have a file now of staff meeting ideas to use in the future!

7

Creativity

The Creative Process

Creativity is our birthright. As children, we lived in the world of our imaginations, becoming absorbed for hours with creative play. We made up stories about our trains, dolls, stuffed animals, or building sets. We romped with abandon, using the vehicles of our bodies to transport us across land, through water, and into the air. We imagined impossible things with "what if" games, and we transcended everyday reality by role-playing action heroes, wild horses, rock stars, or princesses from faraway lands.

As we grew, we discovered other applications of the creative process. We lost ourselves in fictional settings and characters in storybooks. We learned to problem solve and invent. We experimented with paint and crayons, words and language, theories and concepts. We pushed our bodies to and beyond their limits, learning to slide into third base or dance *en pointe* in toe shoes. Some of us discovered the thrill of solving quadratic equations, or executing a perfect backflip, or combining elements in science lab, or building Mother's/ Father's Day gifts in the garage.

As our critical-thinking skills developed in high school and college, we discovered our intellectual creativity and learned to design things with our minds. We learned to take the sheer power of our creative intelligence and manifest it into substance—a term paper, a job, a used car—through good old-fashioned hard work, persistence, intention, and perhaps a splash of serendipity. Many of us undertook the most creative act of all—creating human life, children who grew into miraculous and unique individuals.

We are each experts at creativity, when we think about it!

But over the years, innate creative impulses get layered over with stress and exhaustion. Teaching in classrooms, attending graduate school, undergoing principal training, raising families, and leading a school are each their own creative processes, and paradoxically, they can result in debilitation that keeps us from fully accessing the creativity it takes to be the leader of a school.

In this chapter, let's unlayer the creative self and find out what it needs to thrive and soar.

Warm-Ups on Creativity

I express creativity through . . .

Something I created that I still enjoy is . . .

When I create, I . . .

from Rosemary's journal

I express creativity through *work by designing experiences for staff, parents, or students that are more fun, stimulating, and interesting than what they might expect. I also add a little humor if it works. To thank our project manager after our construction was finished, I photoshopped an orange construction cone onto his photo like a hat . . . it was a big hit. At home, my creativity doesn't have time to be expressed as much. I love to browse art stores and look for books that will stimulate my creativity.*

Something I created that I still enjoy is *from high school. I painted a man and a moose on a huge canvas for an assignment. They both are looking off in a pensive way, and the finished artwork was something that brought a lot of pride.*

When I create, I *like to brainstorm first. The best ideas seem to come the next day, after a walk, or after talking over ideas with others. I also like to cluster ideas and see what pops up. I then move to drafts or sketches or outlines, and then to a final idea/project/plan.*

#20. Creativity Current Reality

What is the current reality of your creativity? Where do you feel juicy and alive? Where do you feel dull and stuck? What creative projects are you working on, or do you want/need to be working on now? Give yourself a "current reality" check-in with your creativity. This can take the form of bullet points, question/answer, narrative flow writing, a character sketch, a story—whatever feels most creative and organic for you.

from Rosemary's journal

Her house has many art supplies, *all hidden away. Dried-up paints for stained glass projects. Colored pencils that are broken and haphazardly stuffed in a diaper-wipe container. Cross-stitch projects partly finished, the stitching disappearing halfway across the canvas. Empty sketchbooks on a shelf. Watercolor pans with broken, chipped circles of color.*

She is an artist inside. Doodling, sketching, and as a teacher, illustrating lessons on the chalkboard and on worksheets. Wildflowers watercolored gently. Wedding invitations handdrawn. Yet time has betrayed the inner artist. Work projects and deadlines are always knocking on the door, demanding to be finished, so the art supplies have dried up. Something inside her creative heart has dried up, too.

#21. Unblocking the Flow

Creativity is a marvelous maelstrom of body, mind, heart, and spirit. If you're feeling creatively stuck, check in with your body. Are you physically tight, cramped, or stuck, as well? If so, unblock your creative flow by getting into motion. What can you do to take care of yourself physically? A hard, sweaty workout at the gym? A long, meandering wander by the river? A Zumba dance class? Yoga? Swimming or running laps? Walking the dog? Massage?

Try this: Choose a workplace situation that is causing some stress, one that you've not been able to advance or pop through. Now choose a physical activity that takes at least thirty minutes. Hold the question or problem lightly as you go about your chosen physical activity. It's also fine to forget about it altogether. When you complete your physical activity, return to the page and write for twenty minutes about the question or problem. You may just be amazed at how your thinking and perception have shifted!

from Rosemary's journal

There has been some friction *between some teachers and specialists about who works with children in literacy and then who is responsible for grades, progress reports, and parent communications. As we have moved into more intervention teachers, children might get all their literacy instruction from someone other than their main classroom teacher. This problem seems to be surfacing more and more. After I let my creative thoughts flow on a two-mile walk, I remembered a time this was happening as a teacher, and it seems to me the same solution may apply here.*

What we did "back in the old days" was have a meeting of the minds. We got all the players around the table. I divided a piece of paper into four squares and listed a role at the top of each square: classroom teacher, special education teacher, classroom helpers, and special education helpers. We listed our roles, responsibilities, and expectations until we came up with a template we all could live with, and then we filled in the squares with our results. This satisfied everyone's need for clarity and gave us a framework for the days to come. It was a successful solution. I'll get to work on it at school with the players involved in literacy instruction!

#22. Creativity Scavenger Hunt

For this fun process, you'll first need to set a dollar budget. Rosemary suggests $25 to $50, although even $10 will work. Next, take yourself on a creativity scavenger hunt to your local art supply or hobby store. (Michael's Arts and Crafts and Hobby Lobby are two chain stores in most communities. Your town or city may have locally owned and operated arts and crafts stores, as well.)

Wander the aisles and see what grabs your attention. Stay within your stated budget; if it's only $10, you can certainly pick up a big box of crayons and perhaps some inexpensive watercolors or colored pencils. For $50, you can get a good inventory of supplies. Rosemary, who now creates beautiful art, says that she was so stifled in her creative expression that she bought a paint-by-numbers kit!

If your creativity is more inspired by motion, go to an athletic store and see what you can find that will help you get and stay unblocked. A jump rope? Hula hoop? Medicine ball? Yoga mat? Stretch bands?

When you're back home again, write about what you bought and how it feels to have taken yourself on an "artist's date" (Cameron 1992).

from Rosemary's journal

Artist's dates are what I need . . . *time to meet, welcome, and embrace the inner artist I have lost sight of. I love office supply stores, always have . . . clean white paper, unlimited shapes and sizes of notebooks, pens of every color, and now even with scents.*

And I love art stores even more than bookstores. I love the idea of possibilities. Possibilities of unlocking the potential within, of having an evening here and there to create, or a project to start and finish, and of the prospect of spending some time in my stifled right brain.

Where to start? My attention is drawn all over the store. Fresh paints, watercolor palettes with moist, tropical colors, brushes of so many sizes and widths I wouldn't know where to begin! I decide to look at some books to activate my brain.

I end up with a book with doodles that need to be finished and a drawing book with activities to improve my sketching skills. That way I can doodle when I have time, add color, and at least have a starting place. My creative brain is so unused it has forgotten how to get started. The drawing book has pages to practice after a lesson, so I can rebuild forgotten skills. I feel like a young child with two presents waiting to be opened. Let the unwrapping begin!

#23. Feeding the Muse

In Greek mythology, the nine Muses were the goddesses of, and were deemed the inspiration for, literature, the arts, and the sciences. Invoking and feeding your muse is another way to get creatively unstuck. As in an earlier process, hold your workplace situation lightly and grab your supplies (crayons, markers, tin of watercolors) and a big piece of paper. Or put on some music and do an interpretive boogie around your family room. Write a poem, one that doesn't rhyme or one that does. Sing at the top of your lungs, or improvise a drum set out of pots and popcorn tins.

Turn your problem inside out and approach it from a different perspective. Find some sort of creative expression, however rusty or imperfect, that will feed your muse and immerse you in a different state of mind. Then, as before, write for fifteen or twenty minutes about your situation. See what emerges. Prepare to be surprised!

from Rosemary's journal

I grabbed my watercolors *and quickly brushed out an impressionistic picture of a woman reading a big storybook to a group. The children's book is to help me remind the staff that we all play different roles for children and yet all have to keep in mind the bigger whole. Too many times, people get caught up in the smaller picture of their classroom or their gym or their music room, and the bigger picture is overlooked. So after calling upon the Muses, I remembered a lesson I had done with a book called* Seven Blind Mice *by Ed Young. The seven mice find an elephant, and each is convinced they have found a pillar, a snake, a fan, or even a cliff. The seventh blind mouse runs all over the shape and realizes it is an elephant. I will read this short, beautifully illustrated fable to my staff and have them reflect upon the parts and the whole. Letting a book send a message is much less painful for them, and it's also a lesson teachers can take back with them to their classrooms. Creativity . . . it's starting to wake up!*

Reflections

What have you learned about yourself and your creativity? Any breakthroughs, "aha" moments, or discoveries?

✍ from Rosemary's journal

My creative side *is stretching and loosening. The creaky muscles are warming up. I am beginning to see that taking time to be creative is critical to my balance and is a piece of who I am. I have always loved art and music, and honoring that part of me will help me keep growing. The musical part seems easy as my husband and I go to concerts, I carry my electronic music with me everywhere and sing out loud in the car often. The artistic part will take some work, yet how much better for me to sketch, or watercolor, or collage in the evening rather than watching TV or working on the computer. I commit to keeping the artistic flame alive!*

8

Communication

Communicating with Self and Others

As a principal, your days are stuffed with communication: teachers, staff, students, parents, the school district, administrators. All day long we receive and process a huge amount of information through careful listening. We practice diplomacy skills as we affirm, critique, and redirect students, teachers, and staff. We juggle difficult communications, ideally without becoming difficult ourselves!

Too often, there's no time left over to really hear ourselves think. And then the workday ends and we go home to families spilling over with news of the day, desire for connection, needs to be met. Or perhaps we go home to a numbed-out silence born of exhaustion.

It can quickly become too much. Yet we know that there is no leadership without constant and effective communication.

Perhaps by now you're starting to understand the value of even five fast minutes of written self-communication. Simple questions like these can offer remarkable insights and directives:

What's going on?
What's the most important thing to do?
What do I need?
What wants to be said?

In this chapter we'll check in with listening skills, practice difficult communications, and learn a terrific technique for checking in with the self.

Warm-Ups on Communication

My communication style is . . .

I wish I could change the way I . . .

from Rosemary's journal

My communication style is *in general to always speak from my heart and be as open as possible. As an administrator, I find I have to constantly run a quick internal check and only say what is appropriate, so my style has become more measured and careful. I still try to be as real as possible.*

I also try to take care to mean what I say and say what I mean. This goes back to the core value of integrity. In all school communications, clarity is probably at the forefront of my mind. How can this email be interpreted? Am I clear? Do I have all the information included so I won't get a gazillion emails asking what time or what day? Have I sounded open? Definite? As I communicate, I'm asking myself a lot of questions!

I wish I could change the way I listen. *I know that in listening there are "techniques" to be a better listener. I wish I had those down more as part of my listening repertoire. One is to set aside your own stories. I still can't resist telling stories, and part of me thinks we are making connections. I am not truly listening, however, as I am trying to relate my own experience. Another technique I learned is to not ask too many questions. I tend to interrupt when I need to clarify. That one makes me crazy when I do it!*

Finally, I wish I didn't always offer solutions. Sometimes I just jump to being the problem solver. Maybe that isn't what is wanted or needed in the moment. I'd like to listen carefully, completely, and compassionately.

____

____

____

____

____

____

#24. The Quality of My Listening

Consider the following categories of people with whom you communicate regularly:

- Close personal relationship (spouse, partner, close friend)
- Workplace peer (assistant principal, department chair)
- Teachers
- Support/resource (secretary or assistant)
- Youth (your own children, students)

Bring to mind a typical exchange with a representative of each group. What is the quality of your listening? How would the person you are speaking with describe it? Write your observations, using phrases such as *I notice . . .* or *I didn't realize . . .*

from Rosemary's journal

Spouse: *I feel talkative with my husband. We both work in management, yet I tend to talk more. This may be that by nature my husband is quieter and less likely to share. I try to ask work-related questions so that I am up to date with his work. I share a lot about problems at work that does not always feel good to me. I would like more balance here.*

Supervisor: *I notice here that I am very tuned in and trying hard to listen carefully. Is there something I might be missing? I also sometimes try to be flattering, which I don't always like in myself.*

Teacher: *I like these exchanges. Usually they are informative, and they feel relationship-building to me. Updates and short bits of personal information are shared. Positive teaching experiences or lessons are shared. Some good news about a child that we're both supporting may be shared. I like to walk around the building and touch base briefly with teachers.*

Secretaries/Office Assistants: *Overall, this is a solid group of people who assist me. There is humor, relationship, and collegiality. There are exceptions. One relationship doesn't feel good to me; our communication is tense sometimes. I feel the power balance is in question.*

Students: *My favorite communications of the day! I enjoy checking in with students. There is no question of power or flattery or balance from my point of view. I try to see what students are learning, if they are having problems, and if there are things I can help with. I notice that at times exchanges with a student can be at a surface level. However, the conversation can go deeper if it needs to.*

#25. Rewriting the Script

There's a funny scene in the old movie *Annie Hall* in which the characters played by Woody Allen and Diane Keaton have a first-date conversation. They make pleasant small talk—subtitled for the audience with angst-ridden, insecure, self-deprecating interior dialogue.

Our communication is often similarly dualistic: Our mouths say words while our thoughts and feelings have an entirely different conversation.

Bring to mind someone in the workplace with whom you have had consistent communication difficulties. Explore what's under the surface that you want to say, but can't. What would you say if you could say anything at all? What's the dynamic here that needs addressing? How can you filter your real message through your core values? What possibilities exist?

from Rosemary's journal

As I started *to work as a principal, I worked with someone who, my intuition said, was not happy with his allotted role in the school and especially not with me. He seemed to think he could do my job and subtly told me so for the duration of my tenure.*

- *"Can I use your office while you are out?"*
- *"Do you want me to write your newsletter for you?"*
- *"How about if I brainstorm some solutions to Problem X, Y, or Z?"*

What I really wanted to say is, "I can do my job. You stick to your job. Back off!!!"

But I didn't know how to address the root problem without being offensive. How do I say my truth? I could state that message over time with some repetition, using the "broken record" approach. I could do some role alignment as mentioned before, and define roles more clearly. I could work toward some understanding of Difficult Person's need for power and perhaps find some areas to delegate. These approaches would be in alignment with my core values.

#26. Dialogue with the Self

Four Types of Journal Dialogue

1. **Persons**—including, in particular, those you're having difficulty with. Also includes aspects of the self (Inner Critic, Inner Coach, etc.).
2. **Body**—illness, stress, body parts (e.g., aching back), Healthier Self.
3. **Work**—the school board, the workload, the role of principal, the faculty.
4. **Inner Wisdom**—the still, small voice inside; the faith-based representation of wisdom (e.g., a parish priest, a guardian angel, a wisdom figure from sacred texts).

Adapted from Progoff (1992)

The dialogue technique (Progoff 1992) is a written conversation in which you write both parts. On the page, it looks like a movie or play script. Once the initial awkwardness dissipates, you'll likely find yourself amazed and impressed with the depth you can attain and the inner wisdom you can access.

In this dialogue process, you'll write a conversation with someone at school with whom you're having a communication impasse. In the dialogue, assume that "that which is highest and best in you" can converse with "that which is highest and best in the other." Bypass the usual communication obstacles (stubbornness, differing agendas, unwillingness to hear another point of

Suggestions for Satisfying Dialogue

- Suspend disbelief. Yes, you are "making it up." It still works!
- Instead of writing what you think, listen internally for what you hear.
- The dialogue process takes time. Allow at least fifteen to twenty minutes.
- Expect surprises. This technique is known for its depth and insight.
- Exit gracefully. When you are out of time, or when the dialogue feels complete, thank your partner and ask if you can speak again.

view) and go straight to the higher and better conversation—the exchange that could happen if one or both of you could set aside the personality factors that hinder effective problem solving.

Begin with closing your eyes and deep-breathing your way into the flourishing zone. Hold lightly the problem, the willingness for solution, and the dialogue partner's presence. Imagine coming together as equals. Silently agree to ground rules of respect and mutual commitment to resolution. Then greet your dialogue partner on paper; say hello. Let your partner respond. Offer a statement of intention, grounded in core values. And let the dialogue unfold.

from Rosemary's journal

Me: *Hello. Just checking in with how you are doing and the vibes I've been getting lately. I feel like you are not happy. I'd like to discuss this.*

Difficult Person (DP): *I really feel that I could do your job.*

Me: *Interesting. Share with me your experience in education.*

DP: *I went to school! I ran a program for a while at another school. I know in my gut all I need to know about running a school.*

Me: *That's great. However, becoming a principal is an entire career path that requires training and experience.*

DP: *You think you are better than me because you have a master's degree.*

Me: *That's not true. However, my education, training, and experience have prepared me to lead this school.*

DP: *I don't feel good about myself so I have to boost my power base and try to gain more power.*

Me: *Hmmm. To me it's more about setting aside personal feelings and focusing on how we work together to get the job done. I really respect your abilities to get things done quickly and efficiently.*

DP: *You do?*

Me: *Totally. I have the utmost respect for your work. You are great at so many things. (I list some.)*

DP: *Oh . . . thank you, I didn't know that.*

***Me:** I should tell you more often. Thanks for all you do.*

***DP:** Well, I respect you, too. You are a really good principal, you work hard, and you know what you are doing.*

***Me:** Thanks! I appreciate that! Meanwhile, I will remember to verbalize and demonstrate my acknowledgment and appreciation of you more consistently.*

***DP:** I am sure that will help me stay focused on being a team player and doing the best job I can for the school.*

***Me:** Let's close for now. Can we talk again in my journal if we need to?*

***DP:** Yes, I would like that!*

Reflections

What have you learned about yourself and your communication patterns? Are there changes or shifts you might address?

from Rosemary's journal

In general, I still believe *in communicating from the heart. This role is complicated. What you say is often repeated and sometimes gossiped about. I need to still remember to focus on clarity, screen myself, and think carefully before speaking. I need to also remember to listen and to be appreciative of others in this role.*

Dialoguing or rehearsing can help with clarity. I can compose emails ahead of time and reread before I send them. All this can help me get to the heart of the matter. And with regard to "Difficult Person," I will definitely remember to convert that imaginary conversation to a real one—to let him know I value and appreciate his strengths and to make a point of offering genuine acknowledgment. I think this will help both of us walk away from a brewing power struggle.

9

Self-Care

Making Time for Self-Care

Who's got time to prioritize self-care when so many other things demand attention, energy, and time?

Who's got time *not* to? Postponing rejuvenation can be costly to health, harmony, productivity, effectiveness, relationships—at school *and* at home!

In this chapter, we'll take inventory of the little things that already serve your self-care. From there, we'll creatively construct a formula for rejuvenation, and we'll have a conversation with your Flourishing Self.

Brew a comforting pot of tea, or pour a refreshing glass of iced sparkling water, and enjoy the indulgence of self-care!

Warm-Ups on Self-Care

My most consistent self-care habit or routine is . . .

I feel depleted and drained in the area(s) of . . .

An idea, project, or solution I continually postpone or ignore is . . .

from Rosemary's journal

My most consistent self-care habit or routine is *walking and lifting weights. I have always enjoyed walking, and with a dog, walking is a necessary part of the day. I decided to learn to work out with weights when I turned forty-five. I had been feeling like I should for many health reasons, most pertinently the danger of osteoporosis and becoming the little old lady in the checkout lane with the stooped posture. I needed some weight-bearing exercise to keep my bones strong. It turned out I enjoy the weights and feel really strong all over after a workout.*

I feel depleted and drained in the area of *feeding my creative side and giving myself some general love and nourishment. I need to nourish the part of me that is starting to feel burned out by taking care of everyone at school. I hear so many issues of health, emotions, social issues, and children's needs that at night I truly feel worn down. Some rejuvenation is needed. This is really about boundaries for myself. How can I say yes to myself?*

An idea, project, or solution I continually postpone or ignore is *the way to move teachers around and hold to my core values. Moving up or down a grade level or two is a huge challenge to some teachers, and many strongly resist change. As a teacher, I valued changing grade levels and became very familiar with developmental levels of different ages. I introduced and taught different curricula and grew personally. In the building I'm in currently, most teachers feel very comfortable where they are and don't want to move. I have been postponing this shift. Now I see that I need to state some expectations and set up guidelines for decision making in this area.*

I need to give plenty of lead time. I will work on a template for how staff and the principal decide how to move teachers, and we'll implement this plan next year. Hmmm . . . that feels good! If I have something on a back burner, it tends to subconsciously nag at me to be solved, and thus it dampens my creativity, productivity, and self-care.

#27. Self-Care Inventory

Complete the Self-Care Inventory sentence stems on the following pages with a word, phrase, or complete thought.

from Rosemary's journal

Overview

My prescription for healthy self-care includes . . . *mind, body, and spirit. Mind: Meditation daily (I'm not consistent). Body: Daily vitamins, cardio, weights. Spirit: Time each day to read inspirational material, time on the weekend to journal. Some boundary setting about what is good and important and meaningful to* me.

To me, taking care of myself is . . . *currently limited to having a physically healthy body. I need/want to devote more time to Mind and Spirit.*

Sensory

An environmental sound or a type or piece of music that soothes me is . . . *Neil Diamond. A guilty pleasure, but his voice settles and grounds me.*

A (reasonably) healthy food that grounds or comforts me is . . . *toast. Toast with soup, toast with jam, toast with melted cheese.*

A book, photo, movie, or piece of art that inspires or calms me is . . . *currently, the work of the author Sarah Ban Breathnach. Her gratitude journal has been a helpful self-care tool.*

A scent, fragrance, or smell that energizes or grounds me is . . . *lilac and lavender. These are scents from my grandmother's garden, and they take me back to my roots.*

A place in nature that rejuvenates me is . . . *outside on the open space trails near my house. Getting out for my daily walk keeps me in touch with the natural world. I started a nature journal last year, and I list in it briefly some weather notes, the hawk that I saw over the field, and coyote or fox sightings.*

Social

The healthy activities, hobbies, and recreation that I most enjoy are . . . *concerts and movies out.*

The friends/family who help me stay healthy are . . . *my husband, Greg. He's just about the world's healthiest person. A snack? An apple! Breakfast? Healthy oat bran, wheat germ, yogurt, and fruit. Weight? Perfect. Exercise? Daily! Okay, he does make me a little crazy, but what a great role model and lifestyle partner.*

Health

The foods that best support my health include . . . *supporting my vegetarian diet with proteins—tofu, soy, legumes, protein powders.*

I sleep best when I . . . *have a fairly clear calendar and am on top of the most pressing "to-do's" on my list, and when I have walked that day.*

My healthiest forms of exercise/movement, and frequencies, are . . . *my daily walk, my visits to the recreation center to work out, and stretching.*

When I am stressed, I want to remember to . . . *take some time out. I need to cultivate an Inner Coach who will shout "Time out for the team!" and a space and time would magically appear for a self-care break.*

For my optimum healthy self-care, I could definitely spend more time/attention/focus on . . . *finding a meaningful spiritual practice. This is still to be revealed. I will pay attention and see what emerges.*

Self-Care Inventory

Overview

My prescription for healthy self-care includes . . .

To me, taking care of myself is . . .

Sensory

An environmental sound or a type or piece of music that soothes me is . . .

A (reasonably) healthy food that grounds or comforts me is . . .

A book, photo, movie, or piece of art that inspires or calms me is . . .

A scent, fragrance, or smell that energizes or grounds me is . . .

A place in nature that rejuvenates me is . . .

Social

The healthy activities, hobbies, and recreation that I most enjoy are . . .

The friends/family that help me stay healthy are (names) . . .

Health

The foods that best support my health include . . .

I sleep best when I . . .

My healthiest forms of exercise/movement, and frequencies, are . . .

When I am stressed, I want to remember to . . .

For my optimum healthy self-care, I could definitely spend more time/attention/focus on . . .

#28. Advice from My Flourishing Self

The journal technique of alphapoems is, as the name implies, a poem that uses the alphabet as a structuring device. The concept is simplicity personified: Write the alphabet, or a series of letters, down the side of the page, and then write a poem in which each line begins with the next successive letter. When you "unhook your brain" and allow your creative imagination to take over, you'll likely be surprised at the ease of writing, and also at the outcomes!

This technique moves quickly. It is best approached by "unhooking your brain" and not thinking too much. Just keep writing. Give yourself seven to ten minutes for a poem using the full alphabet. (By the way, it is perfectly xceptable to cheat on X words!)

from Rosemary's journal

Advice from My Flourishing Self

Advice from My Flourishing Self. She says:
Become more aware of your Self and that you need
Care to grow and
Develop. You need to nourish
Every part of yourself,
Feed your shrunken spirit and
Give attention to your positive mind.
Help your body be the best
It can be.
Just moving through from day to day isn't enough.
Knowing isn't enough.
Loving
Myself
Needs action and decisions and follow-through,
Owning that aging is an ongoing
Process.
Quietly, I commit to
Renewing balance, my
Spiritual, physical, and mental selves
To

Uncover the
Variety of
Worth inside and to
Xplore the
Youthfulness of the inner
Zen that I will create.

Advice from My Flourishing Self

Advice from My Flourishing Self. S/He says:

B

C

D

E

F

G

H

I

J

K

L

M

N

O

P

Q

R

S

T

U

V

W

Y

Z

More on Alphapoems

You can also use alphapoems to burst through a stuck place. Just take a word or phrase representing an issue and write a shorter poem. For instance, you could write an alphapoem in the form of a list that captures the essence of self-care, like this:

Recipe for Self-Care
S unshine.
E xercise, especially walking outside (see: Sunshine).
L aughter! It always helps.
F reedom to express myself and say what I want/need to say.
C hocolate—the fifth food group!
A ttitude: Positive.
R emembering to remember what I know.
E verybody in my support system. Ask for help!

Try your own:
Recipe for Self-Care
S

E

L

F

C

A

R

E

#29. My Self-Care Action Plan

Based on the work you have done in this chapter, what is your current reality about self-care? What is your self-care action plan? What can you put in place, starting now, that will move you closer to your vision of a healthier, more balanced self? This doesn't need to be a major lifestyle overhaul. Just name a few activities, adjustments, or inclusions that you can put into place starting right away.

from Rosemary's journal

An evening routine *to separate from the day and prepare for sleep might help. A look-over at my plans for the next day, a short reading from a calming book, and some gratitude journaling is my plan. Writing three gratitudes each day in a journal my children gave me. It's gone dormant lately. I'll restart and see if this new routine adds some self-care and self-love into my day.*

Reflections

As you reread your thoughts on self-care, what stands out for you?

from Rosemary's journal

Self-care = self-love. *I realize my boundaries are strong elsewhere, but not around this area. If I love myself, self-care should be as natural as breathing. Where is this stranger who loves me? How can I welcome again this woman into my life with time and nurturing? Slowly I'm finding my way back to her.*

10

Wisdom

Keeping a Wisdom Journal

The pace of a principal's life is mind-boggling. Tasks outnumber time slots, deadlines outnumber available hours, individual people have individual matters that all need individual attention, and urgency permeates nearly everything.

There is precious little time, energy, or focus to devote to anything that isn't an immediate, do-it-*now* demand.

That's when the wisdom journal can be wonderfully effective. Spending even five minutes in an alternate *now* reality can bring us back to center.

Wisdom comes from many sources: the elders, teachers, and mentors who have guided us; the teachings and practices of holy books and faith-based communities; our own accumulated life experience; and the still, small voice within each of us that calmly speaks truth.

Among the many ways to keep a wisdom journal is to focus on a quality that will nourish us and offer an immediate injection of ease. We'll explore four of those qualities in this chapter: appreciation, forgiveness, joy, and kindness.

There are many others, of course, and an interesting write would be: *What other wisdom qualities do I want to explore?*

Take a deep breath, center yourself, and layer down to your own inner wisdom.

Keeping a Wisdom Journal: Ten Ways to Begin

1. Keep a notebook or journal with you in the workplace. When you feel yourself starting to frazzle, close your eyes, ask for wisdom, and write for five minutes. Trust what comes.
2. Keep your notebook or journal near your bed at night, opened to a fresh page, with a small flashlight and pen nearby. Should you awaken in the night with thoughts of school, jot down your ideas or worries. Then *close the book* and know that your concerns or brainstorms are captured for morning. This will often help with returning to sleep.
3. Incorporate meditative or prayer writing as part of your regular self-care practice. Set aside ten to fifteen minutes to write. Center yourself with breathing. Let yourself begin with a ritual phrase such as *My heart speaks to me* . . . or *In the silence of this moment* . . . or *Dear God* . . . or *This is what wants to be known.*
4. The Dialogue technique is excellent for accessing inner wisdom. Choose as your partner your own Inner Wisdom, or choose a wisdom figure—a valued mentor, a religious or spiritual icon, or a wise person you admire. It doesn't matter if the dialogue partner is actually available to you. Invoke the essence through closed-eye deep breathing.
5. Immerse yourself in the poetry of ecstatic mystics such as Rumi or Kabir, or of contemporary nature mystics such as Mary Oliver or Wendell Berry, or of contemplative poets such as David Whyte. Write in response to a poem that speaks to you.
6. Keep a prayer or intention journal. You may want to write your prayers/intentions on the right-hand page, reserving the left-hand page for updates and feedback about how the prayer has been answered or deepened.
7. Create a wisdom journal jar or basket. Fill it with a few dozen questions, journal prompts, or quotations from the great teachers and philosophers. Draw a prompt when you're in need of inspiration for a difficult situation. Keep questions open-ended, such as *What is my next step with _______? How can I stay open-hearted? What do I notice about my progress? What do I hear when I listen deeply? What is my next right action? Where does my breath take me right now? What does my soul want from me?*
8. To access wisdom held in the body, write immediately following movement meditation such as walking, dancing, or yoga. Or write a dialogue with your body, or a particular body part.
9. Reread your own writing and watch for patterns, themes, insights, and awareness. Read your own writing out loud to hear nuances of meaning and beauty.
10. Join a contemplative writing circle and allow yourself to be guided into deepened writing, as you are witnessed by others who receive your words without criticism or judgment.

Warm-Ups on Wisdom

The wisest person I know is . . .

In what ways do I bring wisdom to my workday? In what ways do I fail to bring wisdom?

from Rosemary's journal

The wisest person I know is *the woman inside me waiting to be asked questions and listened to. I cover up this wisdom with such noise that she goes deep into the heart of myself and disappears. She is overwhelmed by my inner critic. She knows so much and needs to be brought forth. How can I do this? How can I get realigned with this wise woman? (How have I lost touch with so many parts of myself?)*

In what ways do I bring wisdom to my workday? *I trust in my experience. It is real, it is valid, it is true. I trust in my core values.*

In what ways do I fail to bring wisdom? *Sometimes my good sense is overwhelmed by trying to get consensus from the group. I still don't remember that you can't please all of the people all of the time. I can work on overriding this tendency and relax into the wisdom that I know is present.*

#30. A Note of Appreciation

Appreciation and gratitude are among the most sustaining qualities for thriving. A short, sincere note or email of support and appreciation can make faculty and staff feel heard and acknowledged. And don't leave yourself out of the appreciation cycle! When you're feeling isolated, or standing strong on a position that isn't particularly popular, write a note of appreciation to yourself.

Try it now. Start out, *Dear Principal (your first name), This is a note of appreciation from your wise heart, and I want you to know . . .*

Now try it with another. Bring to mind someone, or a group, with whom you've had conflict or distress recently or presently. Write a note of appreciation. *Dear ______, I want you to know—* You may not want to share this. Or you may!

from Rosemary's journal

Dear Principal Rosemary,

This is a note of appreciation from your wise heart, and I want you to know that inside you is a sage with fine lines of wisdom and life experience etched into her face.

You have lived through a lot; you have raised two children, run a household, mentored others, worked long hours, and built up a lifetime of knowledge. Now you are running a school that nurtures the hearts, spirits, and minds of hundreds of wonderful beings who will grow up to be stronger and more prepared because of your values-based leadership. Do not dismiss yourself lightly. Use this knowledge combined with head and heart, and you will do well.

Love, Your Wise Self

Dear Parent,

This is a note of appreciation from your child's principal. I want you to know that I appreciate how much you want for your child and how you will settle for nothing but the best for your child. You have come to this school because you align yourself with the values here and you truly want your child to have a successful school experience. You know your child best and are your child's best advocate thoughout school and life.

Thanks for supporting our school,

Rosemary

#31. Forgiving Self and Others

Forgiveness is for giving. When you give it to another (or yourself), you release bound-up energy and create internal space for clearer thinking, lighter energy, and brighter possibilities. Complete these sentence stems, and then write a short alphapoem on forgiveness:

- Forgiveness is . . .
- Some people or circumstances I feel ready to release and forgive are . . .
- I don't feel ready to forgive . . .
- I forgive myself for . . .

Forgiveness
I

F
O
R
G
I
V
E

from Rosemary's journal

Forgiveness is . . . *a letting go of the past and living in the present moment. It is tempered by tolerance and is a friend of perspective. It is infinitely kind and generous. It moves in and never leaves. At times it can feel extremely difficult. At other times it is remarkably easy.*

This work requires an attitude of forgiveness. In order to follow my school improvement goals, involve various stakeholders in different aspects of the school, and work toward success, I must let go and move on just about daily. I can't enter a meeting with a hardness or bitterness in my heart. I have to be ready to work as openly as possible. On reflection, maybe that is just called "getting over it" and is the surface level of true forgiveness. Am I doing the daily work of really forgiving?

Some people or circumstances I feel ready to release and forgive are . . . *the people I work with who carry "best intent" in their hearts. These people occasionally let their emotions get the best of them, and yet mean well. In general, forgiveness of small hurts has to happen. I think I am clear that this is a different feeling from whether I trust someone or not, and I will try to start each day with a clean slate as best I can.*

I don't feel ready to forgive . . . *those who criticize and judge and "stir the pot" through power struggles, gossip, and hurtful feedback, particularly those who take refuge in anonymity. It would be so much easier for me to forgive and work it out and move on if "pot-stirrers" would take ownership of their own opinions. Much of this is my sensitivity, but it also violates my core values of honesty, integrity, safety, and respect.*

I forgive myself for . . . *This is a new area of exploration for me. I hold a lot of anger toward myself. I have a lot of faults. I like to be right. I sometimes hold on too tightly. If I can forgive myself, my heart seems lighter and life seems brighter. I am working on it!*

Forgiveness
I *am still hurt, yet know that*
F *orgiveness heals. It is an*
O *utward act that brings*
R *eal peace. When I*
G *ive of myself, I let go and*
I *nner quiet settles in. The*
V *acancy left by tension resolves into*
E *ase.*

____

____

____

____

____

____

Forgiveness Sentence Stems

Forgiveness is . . .

Some people or circumstances I feel ready to release and forgive are . . .

I don't feel ready to forgive . . .

I forgive myself for . . .

Forgiveness Alphapoem

I

F

O

R

G

I

V

E

#32. Captured Moment of Joy

For years, sports psychologists and coaches have known that the subconscious mind cannot tell the difference between something vividly imagined and something that actually happened. Basketball coaches, for instance, have found that players who mentally visualize themselves sinking baskets at the free-throw line perform at least as well as players who stand at the free-throw line and shoot repetitively.

We can use the same power of the "mental game" to bring forward wisdom from past experiences. Because experiences of joy flood our brains with the "pleasure" neurotransmitters, such as dopamine and serotonin, vividly recalling them can help recreate the physiological responses that support happiness and well-being (serotonin) and reward-driven thinking (dopamine).

Find a comfortable position, close your eyes, and relax. Bring to mind a time (preferably recently, but an earlier one is fine) when you felt joy—a sense of lightness, delight, surprise, pleasure, connection. Immerse yourself in the memory and sensations of that time. Feel the texture of the air, breathe in the scents and fragrances, see in your mind's eye the colors and images of the moment, hear the sounds, taste the environment. Focus on the interior experience as well. Name the feelings. When you are ready, write as fast as you can for seven to ten minutes, in the present tense, as if you were right there. Capture the moment.

When you are done, reread your captured moment and write a reflection. How do you feel?

from Rosemary's journal

It is afternoon, *and my husband and I are standing in the "nosebleed" section of the outdoor football stadium, converted for the day into a concert venue. The cold wind is blowing strongly. The sky is overcast. Enviously, we look down on the people below us in better seats, dancing and swaying to the music. The opening band is good, and we enjoy the set, though the wind seems to take the singer's words and distort them and blow them away. Then, U2 comes on. A lifetime of waiting for this moment. The songs are amazing, and the cold seems* *to diminish in the depth of the experience. Then the opening to "Walk On" begins. Bono, sage and wise before his time, begins to sing. The song is so beautiful my heart fills with joy. I put my arm around my husband's waist and he pulls me close, feeling the same way. The lyrics seem profound, and goose bumps rise on my arms. "And I know it aches and your heart it breaks and you can only take so much" . . . ahh. A moment of pure joy.*

#33. A Story of Kindness

"Given a choice between being right or being kind, be kind." That bit of folk wisdom holds a practical secret to flourishing: When we extend small courtesies and kindnesses, the rewards are usually exponentially larger than the effort expended.

Too often, we hold on to stubborn ideas that simply dissolve when we step outside of the right/wrong paradigm and focus on the path of kindness.

Write a short list of times you have been graced with unexpected (and possibly undeserved!) kindness, empathy, compassion, or understanding. Choose one of these times, and write the story. When you are done, reread and turn it around. How did it change you to be blessed with kindness? What is a situation in which a small act of kindness or understanding on your part could change someone's attitude, struggle, or secret hurt? Write that story, too.

from Rosemary's journal

Kindness has touched me *in many ways. Parents stopping by the principal's office knowing exactly the kind of latte I like—decaf, with almond syrup. A tough day and a sweet thank you on my desk from a teacher. A heartfelt handwritten note and illustration for Mrs. Lohndorf, always misspelled, from a student. Kindness keeps me going.*

My new office *is quiet and still. It is late in the summer, hot and dry. I have unpacked my books and set up my computer. I have moved the old, dark, bulky furniture around to make the space look new and refreshed. Then, a tentative knock on the door. A couple and their children, all on bikes, see my lonely car out front, and stop in with snacks. "We wanted to welcome you!" they exclaim happily, arms filled with Gatorade and cookies. "You shouldn't be working in the summer," they continue. "Our friends tell us good things about you. We're glad you are here. Don't stay too late, now." I feel welcomed, nourished, and touched by this gesture of acceptance. Kindness comes on bicycles this day.*

Reflections

What have you become aware of as you have explored the wisdom qualities of appreciation, forgiveness, joy, and kindness?

from Rosemary's journal

Appreciation, forgiveness, kindness, and joy . . . *these qualities are so important.*

It's a positive feeling to bring these to the forefront of my mind, and to put this positive focus on my day. I feel committed to adding more appreciations to the workday for those I work with. They need it. I also am compassionate and kind. These two were things I worked out as a child, as I developed my moral compass.

Forgiveness is a tough one. I have read more lately about forgiveness, and it seems to be something that is a practice rather than a one-time act. There are three parts to forgiveness . . . forgive others, ask and hope that they forgive you, and forgive yourself.

I can make a practice of forgiveness in all three areas.

11

Obstacles into Opportunities

Putting It All Together

In their book *Avoiding Burnout: A Principal's Guide to Keeping the Fire Alive*, Brock and Grady (2002) identify signals of prolonged stress that can lead to principal burnout:

- Feelings of mental and physical exhaustion
- Feeling out of control, overwhelmed
- An increase in negative thinking
- Increased isolation from family, friends, and colleagues
- A sense of declining productivity or lack of accomplishment
- Dreading going to work in the morning (9)

The combination of flourishing principles and reflective practices that you have experienced to this point are powerful tools and natural preventative measures for the early warning signs. In this chapter, we will use what we have learned to tackle an obstacle or issue that has contributed to one or more of the symptoms above.

#34. A Current Obstacle

Bring to mind a current obstacle in your principalship—a "sticky wicket" that needs resolving, yet circumstances, personalities, budgets, or other factors stand in the way of the solution. Perhaps this is even higher than the school building; it could be a "sticky wicket" with your district, school board, or superintendent.

Describe the current reality of the obstacle in some detail. Write candidly about the circumstances of it. Your feelings (frustration, resentment, anger, confusion) may be part of current reality, but they are not the totality. Tell both the content and the feelings of the story. If you find yourself slipping into catastrophizing or overstating, pull it back to rational current reality. Give yourself ten to fifteen minutes, more if you need it.

When you are finished, reread and see if there are immediate insights. Note them.

from Rosemary's journal

For the first time *in my tenure as principal, we have serious budget cuts ahead of us in the spring. There is a timeline for decisions, and the process has been laid out for us. We have to prepare three different scenarios, one mild case, one middle ground, one worst-case scenario.*

The current reality is that we are doing fairly well, in my view. One quality I have with longevity in this district is perspective. I have seen waves of prosperity balanced by waves of cutbacks. It seems that, except for special education, which always is underfunded, we are fairly well-funded. Of course, any cuts will be very difficult. As a district that still works with a semi-site-based model, we get to make all these decisions about cuts at the building level.

As I think about this, several things come to mind: We have to run the budget by all stakeholders and get some type of consensus before sending in to the district; we have to prepare three different scenarios with different results; no one will be happy about any cuts, and even more so if it affects them directly or even somewhat indirectly; and finally, parents, and sometimes staff, tend to look more at personalities than positions. I feel that some positions are critical, yet because the person in the position may not have the best personal skills, the position is now in jeopardy. We have to remember to think about positions and not people.

Insights: *Cutting money and creating a new budget is never easy. There is a lot of work ahead of me. Historical perspective and the future both have to be looked at. There are a lot of meetings ahead of me. A new insight as I write this is that this difficult process could be a positive catalyst for change.*

#35. Applying the Tools

Now, bring to the problem some of the qualities and tools we've practiced so far. For instance:

- What is a core value that could be applied to this situation?
- What is the quality of your listening?
- How might you rewrite the script?
- What is your intention?
- How can you apply creative solutions to this problem?
- What are ideas for moving forward?
- What wisdom qualities would serve in this situation? How can you apply them?

from Rosemary's journal

I now have a whole toolbox *to choose tools from. I notice I feel more confident as I start to think about this process.*

The first idea that comes immediately to mind is a List of 100 as a great tool to start with.

We can list one hundred ideas for cuts with both parents and staff. We could possibly put both groups together for even more creativity and cohesion. As we get down the list and move closer to one hundred it would seem that creativity will emerge and we'll think of ways to cut further away from critical areas.

Also, if we prioritize the list, we can look at lighter and deeper cuts.

Focusing on areas of funding will also be useful. What programs duplicate services? What programs or roles can be filled partially by parent volunteers? What are areas that are protected by laws or statutes?

We can also focus on sources of funding. Are there areas that parent monies could fund? What grants could we apply for?

Listening will be critical during this process. I will remember listening strategies I have learned in management training seminars. Using lists, focused writes, and other brainstorming strategies will help bring openness to the process.

My intention is to maintain the quality of our programming and curriculum, as well as the things that make our school unique. That intention will guide and shape the brainstorming: How can we maintain the essence of our school while reducing costs?

#36. Heart-Centered Communication

Isolate one person (a faculty or staff person, the superintendent) or agency/group (the school board, district administrators, parents) and write an unsent letter or dialogue, remembering the wisdom qualities of appreciation, forgiveness, joy, and kindness. Breathe through it. Stay openhearted and openminded without compromising the essential truth of your position.

from Rosemary's journal

Dear Program Leader,

We are faced with budget cuts. No matter how hard and difficult, this is mandated and has to happen. Because we will have less money to work with, we must find creative solutions to maintain services at the same level. This is our current reality.

I know your program is important. You are a trained, hard-working professional and you have put a lot into your program. You depend on your salary to pay bills and to take care of your family. Please know that you are not alone in your concern.

Our school is alive, full of vitality, and unique. No other school has quite the mix of offerings that we have. I ask you to consider these questions:

- *How can we pull together and make these cuts while keeping our vitality?*
- *How can we depersonalize the process and put all the information on the table to make the best decisions?*
- *Can we agree to put children first? If we make all our decisions around "kids," we will make the best decisions possible.*

Think about these questions and ask yourself where your program could sustain cuts. Thanks for listening and making room for the possibilities of change.
Rosemary

____

____

____

____

#37. Action Plan for Outcomes

Synthesize all of this work into an action plan. What is a first step you can take, starting right now, that will move your current reality in the direction of your intention? What are some next steps? Who can you enroll for assistance? How can you budget time and resources? Make a plan.

from Rosemary's journal

Mantra . . . "Over-inform!"

- *Inform teachers and parents of district information about the budget cuts.*
- *Outline the process.*
- *Create a timeline for the process in line with district mandates.*
- *Create a subcommittee for the budget decisions including teachers, parents, staff, members of the school improvement team, and the school's parent organization.*
- *Generate a mission statement that says children come first and our collective mission is to maintain quality of programming.*
- *Start with current reality for everyone . . . here is the current budget and how it looks.*
- *Show all areas of funding, including parent funds, reserved funds, and more. Disseminate to all stakeholders.*
- *Have a meeting with all interested parties and brainstorm a list of one hundred ideas.*
- *Organize the list into categories and subcategories.*
- *Brainstorm areas of cuts. Organize into areas that most affect children and move to those that least affect children.*
- *Come up with some decisions with a subcommittee and take it to a larger group.*
- *Stick with the timeline as much as possible, and adjust as needed.*

Reflections

What do you notice about problem solving using the principles of flourishing that you have studied and practiced?

from Rosemary's journal

I am truly surprised *by all the ideas that are flowing from this new toolbox. Not only that, but the ideas seem to make sense to me and to be usable. My thinking is broader, wider, and less constricted. The ideas for working with groups seemed to flow, and the action plan wrote itself! A new model for thinking is helping me. I feel less judgmental and more open. I have renewed confidence in my problem-solving skills.*

12

The Flourishing Principal

Flourishing

The labyrinth as a spiritual and reflective tool invites us to take a long, meandering path to a center, pause, and then reverse the pathway to return back from whence we came. Unlike a maze, there are no tricks or dead ends in a labyrinth. To be sure, the path twists and turns, but it is true to its own integrity. When one foot is placed in front of the other, and the path is followed as outlined, the center is reliably reached. Upon return, we bring gained wisdom, insight, or experience to the lives we resume.

The principles of flourishing—connection to core values, balance, realism, intention, creativity, communication, self-care, and wisdom—are similar. As we explore the winding path to each principle through written reflection and contemplation, we arrive at the core of our own strength and purpose, and we bring back to our schools and students the resultant clarity and conviction.

In this final chapter, we will synthesize the learning, create a plan, and celebrate the future as a flourishing principal. Congratulate yourself! You have traveled to the heart of the labyrinth and returned home with the boon of strategies for self-renewal.

Warm-Ups on the Flourishing Principal

As I look back on the experience of writing this workbook, I realize . . .

I never thought that . . .

from Rosemary's journal

As I look back on the experience of writing this workbook, I realize *there is more inside me that needs to be expressed. The Wise Woman wants to be heard, and I am listening. I love the idea of the toolbox that has developed with new ways of inner listening. The ability to access more of myself has increased.*

I can set more boundaries for myself, and I will keep balance at the forefront. As I have worked on all these principles, it has become simpler and easier to state my core values and all that they mean.

I never thought that *a job would be as tough as the one I've taken on. I thought I would be an instructional leader and collaborative decision maker. There is so much more to this work, and I realize that in some ways I wasn't adequately prepared. This process has helped me to see current reality and to fill in the gaps that need to be filled.*

#38. My Flourishing Plan

Let's review your takeaways from the work we have done together. At Figure 12.1 you will find a reprise of the Flourishing Circle we started with. Circle the number that best represents your current standing with each principle, and make some notes about the possibilities—large or small, obvious or subtle—for each principle in your principalship. If there has not been progress in one or more areas, note that, too; it will point you toward your growth edges.

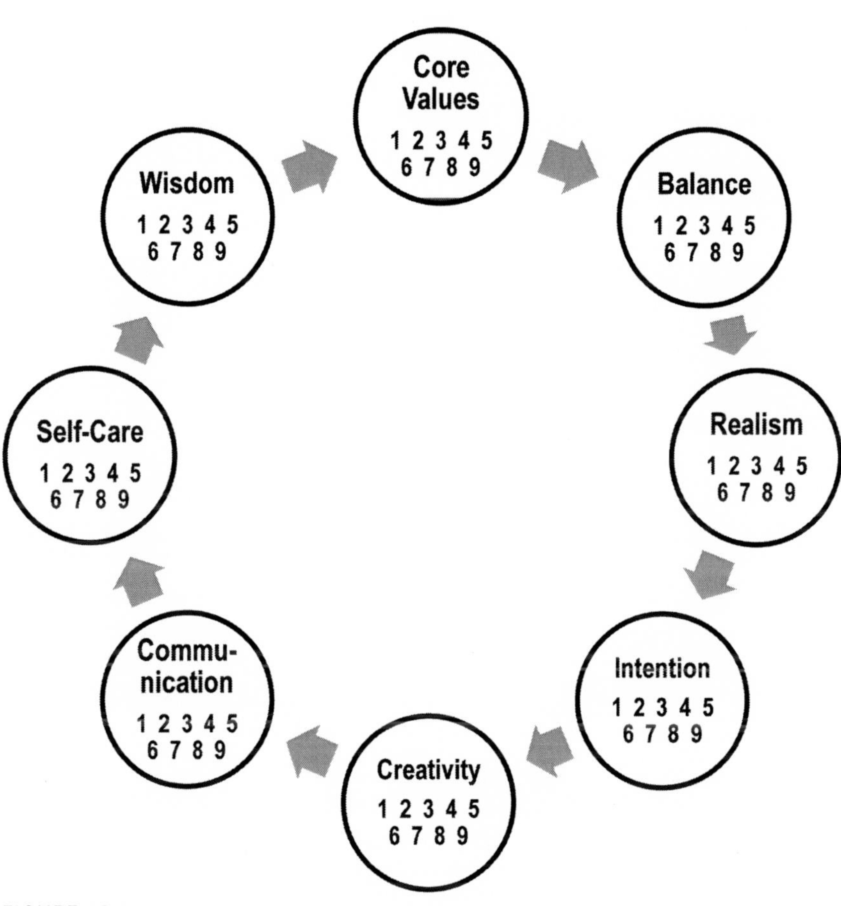

FIGURE 12.1
Flourishing Circle (revisited)

from Rosemary's journal

Core values: *Key to who I am and who I will be. I'm grateful for a leadership program that put good focus on this area. I feel solid with core values firmly planted under my feet. These will continue to guide me in my role as principal.*

Balance: *Balance is being restored to my universe . . . how good it feels to give equal space to other parts of me that have been ignored.*

Realism: *Another grounding principle. If my universe is captured in reality, it can't morph into an alternate universe of large-than-life unrealities!*

Intention: *Holding intentions clear and deep and setting them around a task is helping me move forward with conflict. If my intention is known, other intentions can have room to be heard.*

Creativity: *Creativity is unleashed! Beware the artist inside who wields a paintbrush like a sword, releasing swaths of colorful paint over the blank pages and releasing pent-up cravings for the arts! The release of artistic creativity creates a pathway for creative thinking with problem solving and numerous other day-to-day matters at school.*

Communication: *Clarity, carefulness, and purposeful listening have improved. It has become second nature to check over communications for content, and staff members seem to walk away from conversations with a satisfied look as if they have been really heard.*

Self-Care: *I'm still working on this, and some progress is made over time. Weekly appointments with myself are giving me time and space for growth and development.*

Wisdom: *My trust in myself and in my decisions has deepened. It feels good to acknowledge the wisdom I already have and to know this will continue to grow with experience.*

My Flourishing Plan
Core values:

Balance:

Realism:

Intention:

Creativity:

Communication:

Self-Care:

Wisdom:

#39. One Year from Today

Date your page one year from today. Write as if you are one year in the future, looking back on the year just past. Imagine that you are living your flourishing plan. Many issues and difficult dilemmas have resolved over the past year. Imagine who you have become, how you feel, how you communicate at work and at home, how you balance your life. In addition to writing about what is now your current reality, check in with your feelings, and give some indications as to how the shifts happened (e.g., *It all seemed to turn when I decided* . . . or *Looking back, I can see that it really made a difference to* . . .).

from Rosemary's journal

The principal walks through the building, *sending out appreciations as she tap-taps down the hall. She is confident and vibrates with positive intention. Teachers are working with children and look up to wave hello at the classroom visits. After the walk-through, she heads for a meeting with the office staff. A daily check-in promotes harmonious interactions. Yes, there are conflicts, and honest conversations with good listening skills help get through them. The listening skills have been learned and practiced by all members of the staff.*

Next, a business meeting at the district. All the budget cuts have been implemented, and schools are complimented on their ability to make the decisions with input from all. The future is looking brighter.

Finally, back to the office for the end of the day. As the clock hands get closer to five-thirty, the principal deftly zips through her to-do list, makes notes for the morning, and checks for any last-minute emails. Then she heads out to her car.

On the way home, music changes the mood from businesslike to relaxation. At home, dinner is prepared with more music in the background. After dinner, she enjoys a favorite book.

She muses to herself. Some decisions that emerged from journaling have made room for more balance. Boundaries and parameters have helped efficiency at work and at home. More time is spent equally around the Flourishing Circle. It's the end of a productive day, and the compass is pointing to True North.

References

Adams, Kathleen. 2009. *Journal therapy for mood disorders: A training workbook.* Wheat Ridge, CO: Center for Journal Therapy.

——. 2013. "Expression and reflection: Toward a new paradigm in expressive writing." In *Expressive writing: Foundations of practice*, edited by Kathleen Adams. Lanham, MD: Rowman & Littlefield Education.

Benson, Herbert. 1976. *The relaxation response.* New York: HarperCollins.

Brock, Barbara L. and Grady, Marilyn L. 2002. *Avoiding burnout: A principal's guide to keeping the fire alive.* Thousand Oaks, CA: Corwin.

Cameron, Julia. 1992. *The artist's way: A spiritual path to higher creativity.* Los Angeles: Jeremy Tarcher.

Ellis, Albert and Harper, Robert A. 1997. *A new guide to rational living, third ed.* Chatsworth, CA: Wilshire Book Company.

Frattaroli, Joanne. 2006. "Experimental disclosure and its moderators: A meta-analysis." *Psychological Bulletin* 132, no. 6:823–65.

Fritz, Robert. 1989. *The path of least resistance: Learning to become the creative force in your own life.* New York: Ballantine Books.

Hynes, Arleen and Hynes-Berry, Mary. 2011. *Biblio/poetry therapy: The interactive process, third ed.* St. Cloud, MN: North Star Press.

Pennebaker, James W. 2004. *Writing to Heal.* Oakland. New Harbinger Publications.

Pennebaker, James W. 1989. "Confession, inhibition, and disease." In *Advances in experimental social psychology*, edited by L. Berkowitz, 22:211–444. San Diego: Academic Press.

Pennebaker, James W. and Beall, Sandra. 1986. "Confronting a traumatic event: Toward an understanding of inhibition and disease." *Journal of Abnormal Psychology* 95, no. 3:274–81.

Progoff, Ira. 1992. *At a journal workshop.* Los Angeles: Jeremy Tarcher.

Smyth, Joshua. 1998. "Written emotional expression: Effect sizes, outcome types, and moderating variables." *Journal of Consulting and Clinical Psychology* 66, no. 3:174–84.

Gratitudes

from Kay

I'm grateful to Rosemary for her patience with the process of letting this book reveal itself, her endless good humor, and of course her powerful writes. I'll miss our Thursday morning breakfast meetings!

My friend and colleague Lois Bay, herself a retired principal, offered invaluable insights and perspectives. This book is enriched by her counsel.

To Linda Hendrick, business manager, and Krista Gano, program manager, my deep appreciation for serving as acting directors at the Center for Journal Therapy while I took a writing sabbatical.

Nancy Evans, my editor at Rowman & Littlefield Education, is simply outstanding, and I am grateful for both the freedom and the structure she provides.

My large, loud, and loving family is omnipresent in my gratitudes, and I want to particularly acknowledge my sister and brother-in-law, Cindy and Leo Oury, for the strong and constant principles that have grounded the flourishing of their family.

As always, my ultimate gratitude is to God, from whom all blessings—and flourishing—flow.

from Rosemary

First and foremost I would like to thank Kay for encouraging me as a writer and for inviting me to coauthor this workbook. To write about my passion for education has been transformative.

I would like to express gratitude to my husband, Greg, who has always believed in everything I've done, and who takes me to concerts often. My children, Sara and David, support me too, even though they say they spent too much time rolling chairs down hallways and exploring mysterious parts of school buildings when they were younger.

Finally, a huge thank you to all the wonderful principals, administrators, mentors, teachers, parents, and students I have worked with over the years. All of them have taught me so much. It takes a village.

About the Authors

Kathleen (Kay) Adams is a licensed professional counselor and registered poetry/journal therapist in Denver, Colorado. A pioneer in expressive/therapeutic writing, she is the founder/director of the Center for Journal Therapy, Inc., and its professional training division, the online Therapeutic Writing Institute.

Kay has been a lifelong advocate of the power of writing to heal. For nearly thirty years she has been the voice of journal therapy at conferences, in the media, and in her worldwide work. She is the author of six books on therapeutic/expressive writing, including the best-selling *Journal to the Self* (1990, Grand Central Publishing). As series editor of the It's Easy to W.R.I.T.E. Expressive Writing Series published by Rowman & Littlefield Education, she is the editor of *Expressive Writing: Foundations of Practice* (2013) and this workbook's companion, *The Teacher's Journal: A Workbook for Self-Discovery*, coauthored with Marisé Barreiro (2013). She may be reached through her websites, www.journaltherapy.com and www.TWInstitute.net.

Rosemary Lohndorf, an avid journal writer for many years, is a principal and award-winning elementary school teacher who is recently retired from Colorado's Boulder Valley School District. Rosemary has taught children and adults for over thirty years. She is a certified Journal to the Self® instructor and volunteers as an ESL teacher for Intercambio. In retirement, Rosemary teaches journaling classes, paints, writes, and calls herself a lifelong learner.

Facilitator's Guide[1]

Starting a Flourishing Principal Writing Group

The power of writing is intensified when we gather with others who share a common intention, such as finding creative, effective, and empowering ways that principals might refresh vision and restore balance.

Maybe you've worked your way through *The Flourishing Principal* and have benefited so much that you want to share it with others. Or maybe you're struggling to complete the writes on your own. Maybe you're ready for a structure that will allow you and your colleagues to gather and explore the issues common to all principals. Maybe you just want a reason to gather with friends and write in your journals!

Any of these, and any others you may have, are worthy and valid reasons to start a *Flourishing Principal* writing group. In this facilitator's guide you'll find all the information you'll need to gather some friends and explore your professional lives together. Here's what is included in this guide.

---

1 Adapted from Adams (2009).

- **Ground rules**. I've been teaching the CARES guidelines to facilitators for more than twenty years. It's an effective way to articulate the personal responsibility required for a group to bond. Photocopy the CARES page and treat as a handout.

  In the highly unlikely case that someone does not agree with one or more guidelines, invite further group discussion, problem solve if you can, and agree to speak privately if you can't. If someone cannot come into alignment with one or more ground rules after reasonable negotiation, it may not be the right time for that person to participate in your group. Suggest that you meet six months down the road, and move on.
- **Four stages**. This is for you, Facilitator, as a theoretical context for the facilitation plan to follow.
- **Facilitation planning**. The four stages provide structure and support to the facilitation plan. Here's how we break it down.
- **Facilitation tips and techniques**. Some strategies to help your groups run smoothly, and the master format for your Flourishing Principal group.

After you've carefully reviewed all this material, the most important thing to do is simply to begin. Almost certainly, you have enough of whatever you think you need. You're starting with a well-designed curriculum and easy-to-follow facilitation plans. You already know how to guide individuals to discovery. You don't have to do this perfectly. Why wait? Let's write!

This Group CARES!

Every group benefits from common-sense agreements that will keep the group experience comfortable and accessible for everyone. By agreeing to these ground rules, each individual acknowledges personal responsibility for a shared vision of respect, trust, and safety.

Read the ground rules for the circle. Discuss any questions. Then ask: "Does everyone agree to the CARES guidelines? Please raise your hand and say 'yes' if you do."

Confidentiality. We are each empowered to talk about our own experience within this group with anyone. We each agree not to talk about anyone else's experience without the other's specific permission.

Acceptance. Our stories are diverse and rich. They have shaped us. We accept our own stories and the stories of others detached from judgment, critique, or the need to fix or resolve.

Respect. We respect the integrity of the group by arriving on time, staying the entire time, notifying the leader if we will miss a session, and not monopolizing shared time. We respect each other by listening attentively and compassionately. We refrain from interrupting, side talking, critiquing, or debating.

Expression. We take authentic self-expression in its many forms, which might involve tears, swear words, mundane thoughts, radical ideas, or other forms. We gently remind ourselves and each other that we do not need to apologize, we are not taking too much time, and our expression matters. Balancing that, we are mindful of the context in self-expression, and we respect social boundaries and the confidentiality of our workplaces.

Self-management. We agree to participate at the level that we are able, and we are aware that we have full permission to decline or change any invitation, suggestion, or instruction.

The Four Stages of Expressive Writing Groups

In their classic book *Biblio/Poetry Therapy: The Interactive Process*, third edition (2011), Arleen McCarty Hynes and Mary Hynes-Berry outline a four-stage model for expressive or therapeutic writing groups. This is the flow of the individual session. Over time these stages, and their accompanying rituals, reveals, surprises, and treasures, become "the writing group," an experience infused with authentic expression, authentic connection, hope, and strength.

First: Recognition

The recognition stage allows each participant to place himself/herself in the group. Through warm-up exercises and initial sharing, group members identify with the theme of the group and self-select into participation.

Second: Examination

The recognition stage deepens into examination of the themes and issues that surface for each group member through written exploration and reflection. Structured writing prompts are offered to focus and jump-start the writing process.

Third: Juxtaposition

The juxtaposition stage is characterized by two or more ideas, expressions, moments of awareness, or/and interpretations placed next to each other so that comparison/contrast can expand each. Juxtaposition routinely occurs during the sharing portion of an expressive writing group, when a group member's universe of thought and process expands as she or he compares and contrasts another's experience, beliefs, worldview, and more with her or his own. Juxtaposition also often happens within the write itself through bumping up against the natural push/pull of expressive writing: "I feel this way, but I also feel that way" or "I want this, even though it's probably not in my best interest."

Fourth: Application to Self

The last stage, application to self, allows group members to take away and apply learning from the group. The facilitator supports this stage by offering a reflection write for the session as a whole, or a closing verbal round of "What is my takeaway from this group?" or "What have I learned that I can use and apply?" The application-to-self stage might also be supported by suggesting follow-up writing processes to do between group meetings—perhaps the remaining chapter prompts that were not used in the group itself.

As with most linear models, the stages of group process are not discrete and segregated but blend into one another and may be experienced simultaneously. However, the stages do tend to present in order. The facilitator's tasks are to structure processes (warm-up, discussion questions/main write, synthesis) so that the natural order of the four-stage model can organically emerge, and to facilitate the dialogue and sharing in a way that encourages the fulfillment of tasks for each stage.

Facilitation Planning

An expressive writing group typically consists of a warm-up, perhaps a short teaching, a main write, a sharing/process round, and a closing. Here's how a *Flourishing Principal* group would use the Hynes and Hynes-Berry structure.

Warm-up (the Recognition stage)

- Helps move the participant from "out there" to "in here"
- Can be either verbal or written
- May (but does not have to) preview the content of the session
- Facilitator may participate in verbal warm-ups for role modeling
- Use whichever warm-up you prefer from each chapter of *The Flourishing Principal*, or offer more than one as "writer's choice"

Teaching (Recognition, Examination, possible Juxtaposition)

- Ties the writing process to an outcome or goal
- Instills knowledge and/or awareness

Main Write (Examination, Juxtaposition)

- Specifically targets the session's outcomes or goals
- May be preceded by brief guided imagery, entrance meditation, or guided relaxation and focusing, led by facilitator
- Lasts ten to fifteen minutes, depending on capacity of group and length of session

- It is very helpful to invite rereading and brief reflection (*As I read this, I am aware of* . . . or *I notice* . . . or *I am surprised by* . . . or *I'm curious about* . . .) after each main write. This immediately anchors fresh insight, discovery, and awareness.

Sharing (Examination, Juxtaposition, Application to Self)

- Sharing is always optional, and always encouraged.
- There are several ways to share:
  - Read what was written
  - Share the brief reflection write in lieu of the write itself
  - Talk about what was written
  - Talk about the process of writing
  - Pass
- Unless there will be time for specific process comments for every write, limit comments to simple acknowledgment plus a generalized comment, such as:
  - What is it like for you to read that out loud?
  - Are there any surprises for you?
  - Is there a word, phrase, line, or idea that calls to you?
- When someone shares surprises, insights, "aha" moments, and more, the facilitator can offer those back as writing prompts, to be completed between sessions.
- In an expressive writing group, sharing is *never* about receiving "critique." The facilitator/volunteer leader is responsible for setting this ground rule early and redirecting critique behavior.

Closing (Application to Self, New Recognition)

- If there is time, offer a very brief (three to five minute) synthesis write to bring it all together ("What I learned . . ." or "What I am taking away . . .")
- Close the group with a group poem (one line from each person's write), a closing thought or quote, or a closing word or phrase ("Say a word or two that describes how you're feeling right now" or " . . . something you learned tonight" or similar)
- Offer writing "homework" if appropriate
- Remember that you're winding down, not ramping up, so be mindful of not asking provocative or process questions at the closing stage

Facilitation Tips and Techniques

- In a formally facilitated group, the facilitator does *not* participate in writes (even if facilitator plans not to share) because the facilitator's role is to hold the container of the group and be the guardian of the process. In a less formal group, such as a gathering of peers coming together to work through *The Flourishing Principal*, the leader may choose to write with the group. However, since the facilitator is also the timekeeper, it's actually easier if the leader writes in advance.
- When you complete the instruction to write or/and the entrance meditation, give a time orientation: "We'll write for about ten minutes, and I'll let you know when there's [one or two] minutes left." Then give a one-minute (writes of seven minutes or less) or two-minute (writes longer than seven minutes) time cue: "One more minute," or "Take about two minutes more." If you want to add the instruction to read and reflect at the end, bring the writing process to a close, and then give three or four more minutes for reading/reflection.

- Here's a little tip to help you keep track of time. When you say, "We'll write for (some) minutes," jot down the time like this (for a ten-minute write):
  - Start writing: 7:00
  - Time cue: 7:08
  - Stop writing: 7:10
  - Read/reflect: 7:13

Or you can shorthand it like this: 7:00→7:08→7:10→7:13

- Point out ideas or insights from each person that could become prompts for writes between sessions.

- Some facilitators like to use a "talking piece" to signify whose turn it is to speak or share. The talking piece can be anything from a stone to a coffee spoon; it ritualizes the sharing process and protects the one sharing from interruption. Talking pieces are best introduced in the "ground rules" section of the first meeting. As facilitator, you will explain the convention that the person who has the talking piece has the floor; everyone else offers active listening and holds silence until invited to speak.

- Make sure to note at the beginning of any "talking piece" round that anyone who is not yet ready to share may pass the designated object, and it will come back around a second time for those who passed. Sharing is deemed complete after the second opportunity. Note that this is not invitation for those who have already spoken to speak again, unless you have allotted time.

- In general, the hardest shift that classroom teachers (and perhaps principals, since so many were formerly classroom teachers) report when moving to a facilitator model is the awareness that they are not expected to have answers, resolve questions, or make things happen. As facilitator, your responsibility is simply to introduce the concepts, guide participants into their journals through the writing prompts, and facilitate sharing and witnessing. It is tremendously powerful and rewarding work, but a common response is, "It doesn't feel like I'm doing anything!" Be assured: Creating a safe container for deep work to happen is "doing something." If it feels effortless, so much the better!

- Each of chapters 2 through 12 makes a stand-alone group. I recommend 1.5 hours per group if you can manage it. Adaptations for a one-hour group are also included. If you have two hours, you can build in time for social conversation and/or deeper discussion and process after the writes. The timing for a sixty- or ninety-minute group goes something like this:
  - 0:10 Allow up to ten minutes past start time to gather, greet, settle in. Start earlier if you can.
  - 0:15 Five minutes to do a brief verbal check-in round—"something you'd like to share about your week" or "report a piece of good news" or similar. Keep this very focused by instructing "one or two sentences" or "no more than a minute each."
  - 0:25 Offer one or more warm-up writes from the chapter, with the instruction to write on *only one* for two to three minutes. Then go around the circle and share. This might take up to ten minutes for a ninety-minute group, but keep it to five minutes for a one-hour group.

  In a ninety-minute group, you'll have opportunities for two longer writes/shares. Decide in advance which two processes from the designated chapter you would like to offer. If you are doing a one-hour group, you'll only have time for one longer write/share.

- 0:30 Read/describe from the workbook chapter the first process, and ask for questions or clarifications. Lead an entrance meditation if you choose. Advise the group that they will have a set amount of time (usually seven to ten minutes) to complete the write. Give a one- or two-minute time cue at the appropriate point.
- 0:40 Bring the writing to a close, and invite sharing for about fifteen to twenty minutes. It's fine to ask some follow-up questions or to invite a little bit of process conversation.
- 0:55 If it is a one-hour group, bring sharing to a close and invite reflection on the session. Use the prompts from the Reflection page in the chapter. If it is a ninety-minute group, wrap up sharing and introduce the next writing process. Ask for questions or clarifications. Continue as before, leading an entrance meditation if appropriate and letting participants know they will have seven to ten minutes (usually) to complete the write. Give a time cue at the appropriate point.
- 1:05 Wrap up writing and invite sharing, as above.
- 1:20 Transition into reflection writes for three to five minutes.
- 1:25 Invite a closing round of sharing about reflections or takeaways.
- 1:30 Adjourn until next time!